True Stories from a Pastor
Always in a Pickle

TimHill

About the Publisher

McKnight & Bishop are always on the look-out for new authors and ideas for new books. If you write or if you have an idea for a book, please e-mail us at:

info@mcknightbishop.com

Some things we love are undiscovered authors, open-source software, Creative Commons, crowd-funding, Amazon/Kindle, social networking, faith, laughter and new ideas.

Visit us at **www.mcknightbishop.com**

ISBN 978-1-905691-67-8
A CIP catalogue record for this book is available from the British Library

First published in 2019 by McKnight & Bishop Inspire, an imprint of:

McKnight & Bishop Ltd. | 26 Walworth Crescent, Darlington, DL3 0TX
http://www.mcknightbishop.com | info@mcknightbishop.com

This book has been typeset in Arial, American Typewriter & All Over Again.

Printed and bound in Great Britain by Cloc Book Print Ltd

I would like to thank Mark McKnight for his
encouragement and work on this book.

To all of us who are stalked by humbling reality checks!

It's the natural direction to go – but why should I get someone else to write it? That seems to be the way: The Archbishop of Canterbury says this, comedian Andy Kind says that, well I could ask Justin or Andy, or my MP, they are all lovely people but let's just get on with the book eh? It doesn't really matter if they like it: I just hope you do!

I'm tempted to leave in spelling mistakes and bad punctuation, because it reflects me. I'm inconsistent, always have been, oops, that would be consistent! Ok well most of the time I'm inconsistent.

This is a gathering of real experiences into one year. The place names have been changed as have some people's names, just to protect them. Instead of a cast of thousands, some happenings have been loaded onto the key characters. It's not an actual year then, but you could try and date it by songs or events and technology – a pointless effort worthy of the much coveted Pointless trophy should you manage it!

So that's the Forward then – launching us like an Introduction towards the beginning of the story – my manic life. We start in

September because the school year starts there and my wife and I are tied to that.

Backward

Hang on! I quite enjoyed writing the snappy little Forward. So I thought about a Backward. Then I got to wondering why Christian Ministers are always going on Spiritual Retreats! They should be going on Spiritual Attacks – that's what I'm on and have been pretty much all my life. My aim has been to raise God's profile and get people one step closer to Him. The mishaps that go on around me? Well, some are my fault and some are just 'life' – it seems like it's out to get me sometimes but it's not, some of us just bump the edges of it more than others.

So is this book a rant? or a handbook? Or what? – well it's just some autobiography in condensed form – in a little blue and white striped tin if you like (surely condensed Milk is 'Mlk'?!) (and surely 'surely' should be spelled 'shuerly'?!). I asked my mum when I was about 9yrs old who was in charge of spelling because I thought they were doing a very poor job! She told me it was the government. I felt the urge to write to someone but didn't know who. Now I know who, and I know they wouldn't understand. In fact the government can't change stuff like that anyway, looking at our present bunch that's probably for the best. Or for the 'bst' once the Minister for the Environment has removed the ‘E’s. BuDumTish. The ‘B’ has to go too – most have died so I read, very sad! We are left with ‘st’ then – that’s only a word in Scrabble type games. I’m taking the ‘t’ out now, I react badly to tea and coffee and it was starting to make me feel ill.

So that done, I think it’s ‘s’ if I get started with the traditional Chapter 1. How conventional am I?!

1. A New Hope

(Which is secretly Part 4)

Getting the job as Church Community Evangelist was great in many ways: we didn't have to move far, the church seemed forward looking and the house they provided was bigger than anywhere we'd lived before. The pay wasn't great, it was based on the average earnings of the Deacons (if it was based on the average earnings of the elders I'd be on twice as much!) which kind of told me where I stood in the pecking order.

Fortunately my wife was earning more and together we pulled in a decent amount: this was good as we could give a good tithe and Mandy could still buy shoes when she fancied (they help her teach apparently).

The arrival in Basley with a lorry load of boxes and furniture was conventional. I returned the van to Boscombe the next day and stopped to get a kebab before driving my car up to our new home with the last few bits in it. The kebab had some unwanted effects and I spent the next 2 days on my back (though at times I believed I was on the ceiling!) and when I came round several realisations hit me hard a) the furniture had moved itself into nice positions; b) the cupboards were stocked c) there was a smell of fresh paint. Mandy and some church members had managed without me. Oh, and d) I should get a duster and remove the cobwebs from the ceiling. [Interestingly most Vicarish type people don't look up much. If they did they'd see the cobwebs on their ceiling! Go on now, take a break and visit your local Manse. Back already? But I was right wasn't I!?!].

I recover from illness and accident quickly, a good trait as the next will be just around the corner. Working in schools tends to lead to a cold every 7 weeks or so and visiting the sick (when I'm well) ensures I'm topped up with bugs even during the holidays. It's ok to complain about all this – I'm Welsh, or used to be.

We Welsh are a people born to complain. In our version of English we have a generic term 'they' for the people who do things to us that we deem wrong or complicated. So 'they' put the taxes up, 'they' didn't collect the bins, 'they' arrested my maths teacher and 'they' can't spell (see Backward). Have a go today, and if you don't enjoy it, blame 'them'. Complaining is fun and is the basis of much stand-up comedy thus the success of the brilliant Rhod Gilbert.

I had recently recovered from the trauma of a holiday in Cornwall – that was 'their' fault too. My ever loving and highly organised sister had booked us all (my father, his friend, my sister and her family) into a Christian Endurance Holiday Home. A dilapidated mansion run by an arrogant grump, it had no en-suite rooms, lopsided furniture and a stand-in chef we couldn't stand. We were bossed about when we parked and bossed about every day in various officious ways until we left a week later. We were tired and wanted a break, what we got was stress and disappointment.

The toy trunk was the first port of call for our daughter Alice when we arrived in the vast hallway – but the box was empty bar for a dolls arm – oh! The tears! When I stopped crying I saw that Alice was upset too. Hideous paintings were all over the huge house, kind gifts from grateful residents apparently. The games room seemed like a reasonable retreat for lads young and old... nothing like shooting some pool and pinging some pong. But the games room was in the garden – a rotting summer-house with uneven floors, broken windows and incomplete sets of balls. The Ping-Pong ball had to double as the 'white' for pool. The table tennis table had a mossy patch which hampered play, as did the hole in the floor at one end and the hole in the roof at the other.

I complained to the pompous Manager that Health and Safety should close the games room – but he insisted that people must be allowed their fun. I had interrupted him during a telling off of some teenage boys who had been heard laughing. Shame on them. He insisted there would not be a repeat of this and they should go to their rooms by ten o'clock like everyone else (not hard to comply with as there was actually nothing to do! No film nights, no quizzes, no disco or band... nothing).

Anxious as I always am to improve people's lives, I offered to host a variety show on the last night. Before the managing twit could say no several holiday-makers said yes, and there was no stopping it!

The week staggered on with poor food, poor weather and disintegrating furniture (our bedroom chair collapsed and a leg came off a wooden cupboard type thing) so we Welsh had a wail of a time complaining. Cheered by that and the hope of a fun finish on Friday night, we failed to notice the option of suicide.

The variety night was planned by me, a weave of music, joke-telling and sketches, and mentally I set the bar of expectation low. As all sat down and I introduced myself, a horrible realisation hit – people were staring at me with hard frowns that defied me "go on then, try and make me smile, you'll not manage it!" Oh dear. I tried jokes that usually worked – they didn't. I tried a sketch but the person I chose to read with me had no comic timing at all and killed a classic making me want to weep. Then the moment I dreaded: someone had asked if they could recite 'Albert and the Lion'. That's as old and cheesy and as low as any comedy night can go but I said yes because I couldn't say no. After the faulting rendition, with the dreadful fake Yorkshire accent and a few polite laughs, the volunteer sat down. Before I could speak another chap jumped up and recited the same poem! I was flabbergasted. No-one laughed and yet he sat down with a contented smile!

As I rose to not thank the two performers, a hand went up in the audience. The pasty man who all week had talked to every family about how he and his wife couldn't have children (and then individually confided to everyone that it was his wife's problem not his) rose and through tears said that he too would like to recite Albert and the Lion! And he did, except that he couldn't and so large chunks were missing, making nonsense of the storyline. He sat down to stony silence and I gave up on any form of fun with this crowd of out-of-date, stuck-in-the-mud miseries – I rose to my feet, raised my glass of water, tipped it over my head and walked out.

As I said, by September I'd recovered from that, no lasting stain on my memory, no bitterness. Just £600 wasted and I never want to holiday in Britain again.

Mind you, disasters can happen abroad too… I must mention our honeymoon some years ago…

Mandy was then my girlfriend and she did know what she was letting herself in for. We talked about church work and possible poverty and sacrifice and even the probability that we'd end up in Japan as missionaries. I couldn't put her off.

She was pretty and intelligent and could have easily worked out that while I was confident in-front of a crowd, I was inept and lacking confidence in private. I had to be pleased though, punching above my weight like that. So we went to a travel agency and gave them the date of our wedding and the budget.

When they had stopped laughing they offered us a coach trip to our chosen destination that was as close to our budget (not close) as they could get – but it was for the week before our big day. I pointed this out to the girl who cheerfully explained that we would still make it to the wedding because the coach returned on the Saturday morning, and the service was in the afternoon! How stupid I felt, I hadn't thought of that, typical me.

I got a little annoyed actually, unusual for me, and said that the Honeymoon had to follow the Wedding (I have a trait of conventionality) – and we booked a holiday, not exactly what we wanted but it began the day after the wedding so that was something.

The Honeymoon began in a hotel which had bullet holes by the front door – parts of South Wales are rough! We travelled by coach next day and by nightfall we were in Brussels looking for the Novatel, we found it at about 2am – the driver was actually lost but wouldn't admit it. The next day we drove to the Alps and the bus pulled up outside a pretty half-timbered Chateau complete with colourful window boxes, slatted shutters and all just across the road from the Lake – awe-inspiring! The driver went in, returned five minutes later and drove us off into the night. Apparently there had been a double booking, our hotel was full and we had been given an alternative. We arrived at the alternative just before midnight and were welcomed by a fierce bullish hag who spat German instructions at us and would not allow umbrellas or anything else wet to go upstairs. With no lifts, porters or other help we trudged our weary way up stairs, hundreds of them, until we found our room. There was no toilet but we were reassured that the green plastic coffin in the corner was actually a shower! Our room was in the roof and had little furniture, three single, cot-sided beds, screwed to the floor and one shutter between our three windows (and that was hanging off).

How bad could it be? The food was plain and portions were tiny. One day my meal was a small circle of pork, ten chips half a tomato and a hard-boiled egg. My wife was given the same so pointed out that she was vegetarian (with exceptions too complicated to explain in a single volume book) – they withdrew her platter of delight and returned after much obvious toil – presenting her with a plate that now only contained ten chips, half a tomato and a lump of cheese. Such culinary skill cannot be taught I suspect.

After each meal all the holidaymakers would form an orderly queue to complain to the Courier. Most berated her, condemned the holiday company, demanded compensation and bemoaned the lack of tea.

After two days, that's six queues of 42 complainants, she had a breakdown and was not seen again. A replacement came 2 days later and got the same treatment. One man, Paul, said his room was next to the road and overlooked the garden (which was a concreted area with a Petrol pump in the middle of it) and that it was so noisy he couldn't sleep. They moved him to the annex of another hotel, one normally only used in the skiing season and therefore ghostly quiet at that week in August. That evening he told us of the big comfy bed and the luxury compared to our (alleged) hotel. We all thought of applying to move in there. Next morning at breakfast a bleary eyed and very emotional Paul told us about the main rail-line from Germany to Italy and how it runs next to his window and the ruthlessly efficient timetable which allowed 12minutes of slumber between each express train. You've got to hand it to the Germans eh?

Those surviving the week long ordeal were not surprised when the coach broke down at Calais or the howling gales that greeted us when at last we reached Blighty.

Still at least we didn't end up in hospital as we have on so many other summer holidays. And I didn't get arrested… tell you about that another time.

On with September then. New house, new job, all healthy, friendly church people and an Indian summer. All good then. There are some points in life you'd just like to stop in aren't there! I'd stop there I think.

The first few weeks were full of invitations out to meals and we got to know families and children and lots about the town. It was an overspill from London really, any original features were under car-parks now and yet it boasted wonderful fast food outlets and take-aways from every area of Asia.

One meal in a Chinese restaurant with a lovely family ended in disaster when the big circular table we were sat around tipped onto me. This would not have happened if the back legs had not come off my chair, but that happens a lot. I grabbed for the edge of the table as I went down and people opposite me saw their plates suddenly rise past their faces! What they then could not see was the food sliding to the floor opposite them, where I was now sitting. We didn't go back there.

One of my first Pastoral visits was to a lady in a thatched cottage on the edge of town. I'd heard she was in a tizzy and saw it as a good opportunity to help. I live to help. Go on, just ask me. Arriving in the driveway I was met by the flustered and slightly squawky lady who in her posh excited tone and with no few tears told me of her upset and the stress and confusion – but I didn't get the gist. "What is actually the problem?" I asked firmly after allowing the squawk too much rein, "Well it's the third time the fabric consultant has been and I still don't know whether the valances should match the curtains!" I looked concerned (to hide the relief and the desire to laugh) and said, "best go for plain". And I left. Fabric Consultant?! It that even a real job?

My Senior Minister at Church was an elderly scot who called all women pet and imagined the best in everyone. He said I was doing fine every week when we met up to discuss and pray about the week's events. He let me preach once a fortnight and I gave my best sermons with enthusiasm. What would I say though next month?

As well as visiting people during the week I got involved in the local schools and took at least three assemblies per week. Add to that some lessons, some private study and a theology course in London once a week and you'll understand why there was hardly time to prepare for the live radio show each Thursday afternoon, or write the regular newspaper articles or visit at the town Mall where I was a Chaplain.

Sometimes I would take my daughter with me if she was not in school, and what a delight she was! Everyone was glad to see her and her manners were pretty good too, leading to lovely compliments and lots of hugs. What always baffled me was the journey in the car to visit people who were 'out'. She seemed to know! We would set off and she would ask "Where are we going?" I would reply with a name like "We're going to call on Pat and Brian" and she would pause then volley back "they're out". And she was always right. Weird.

Our first few weeks flew by and the house rapidly became home. I upset the neighbours a few times (having a bonfire at mid-day, owning a bright yellow ex-BT estate car which apparently "brought the neighbourhood down" and spraying my garden fence blue but in the process changing the colour of many of the plants locally) but made friends too. We started up a Neighbourhood Watch and I was happy to be Chair of that as my time was more flexible than most.

I also got the chance to visit some of the other churches in the town. One old chapel had asked if I could do some evangelism with them to bring the locals in. I said I would need to visit first and then pray about it. Their only weekly activity seemed to be a 3pm service on Sundays so obviously I went along. The lady I had been corresponding with was Edna and she met me and introduced me to her friend Marj.

We sat in the white-painted wooden building that had once been a barracks and waited. And waited.

I was about to ask when would the others come when an old gent, bent and grey, tottered in from the vestry and took his place in the pulpit. Edna rose, bedecked as she was in a camel hair overcoat and black beret (allowing lecherous men to gaze on just a 2inch area of alluring flesh – she said her mother had warned her about men. She had never married and was now 78) and shuffled up to the organ.

That left Marj and I in the congregation. Edna hit a note and we all rose (!) for the first hymn. Eric Morecombe's wonderful argument with Andre Previn came to mind (go, Google it now!) but by the second verse I'm not sure Edna was actually playing all the right notes let alone in the wrong order!

The old gent running the show barely moved, I'm not sure there was much movement left in his stiff skeletal body. At the end of the hymn he prayed in pre-Shakespearian English and read from a pre King James Version of the Bible. Any movement as he looked down at the pages of scripture caused a small snow-flurry of dandruff. I guess the book must be full of it by now. He announced a second hymn and stood back in fear. Edna false started the tune several times, her unseen legs pumping away at the old organ. As the pedals pushed air into a bellows and she hit various notes, I began a personal game of 'name that tune'. I failed.

The sermon was mumbled, archaic and the long pauses this Victorian gent was employing simply made me think he had died each time. It ground on and a dog wandered into the back of the chapel, looked around, saw there was nothing going on and walked out – such wisdom in a dog!

Definitely a glutton for punishment the old guy announced a final hymn, I stifled a laugh. I was actually looking forward to it! I wasn't prepared for what happened next though: Edna shuffled to the pump organ, failed to find the tune several times, stood up, announced to no-one in particular that she couldn't play that tune on the pump organ and shuffled to a previously unnoticed

Hammond electric organ! There was a loud click as she switched it on and a hum thereafter. Her ineptitude undiminished but with several tones to choose from, she made a stab at the well-known hymn and I thought for a moment we were going to be able to sing to it. Then the familiar combination of notes was gone, the hum increased and she gave up. Throwing her hands up in horror she shuffled back to the pump organ and tried again. We threw her a bone – singing despite her rather than with her and then it was over.

As we left, the old preacher approached me and dandruff fluttered before my eyes. "So you're the chap who is going to do some evangelism for us are you? I've been a trustee here for over 50yrs" (he said proudly). I replied "I'm the chap Edna contacted, yes, but what I can do for this church? Well, I suggest you offer it to the National Trust as it used to be a barracks, they might be interested". He explained that the chapel had been in place for 200yrs and they didn't intend closing it. "Then you must have a rescue plan for it?" I said, to which he replied with the immortal get-out clause in Christian circles "But how should'st we know what the Lord would'st have us do unless He reveal it unto us?" I was getting annoyed, "Well you could approach two or three local growing churches and ask them to prayerfully send 2 families each to re-start the fellowship here"

"That's a thought" he stated. "That's a thought you should have had ten years ago" I stated back. I then suggested he let the two old ladies go to the vibrant local churches I mentioned where they could get proper pastoral care and real fellowship. Bless them for continuing in their labours for so long, but they were missing the whole point of church! Failed fellowships like that are largely unnoticed by the public but where they are observed, it's a negative impression they leave. Its tradition only and it shoots itself and the rest of Christianity in the foot!

It's like churches that have large white notice boards with black gothic lettering. No matter how new and pithy the message, the image shouts 'CREEPY' at passers-by.

I think that chapel did close and both ladies have moved over to better churches, chapels blessed with people and musicians.

Visiting churches and schools I soon became known in the area and when walking along the shopping streets in town, children would often yank at their parent/guardians arm and point "That's Tim!" I would hear it and say hello to the adult then to the child and a conversation would ensue. The usual outcome would be that the child would tell me about a song I taught at their school and/or a trick that I did and then the adult would ask which church I was attached to.

A notable assembly early in my time at Basley concerned mini-beasts. That's a topic the infant schools seem to cover in Autumn Term so I would helpfully do an assembly with a God-spin on Ants. The key to Assemblies as to most things is "Inform, Challenge, Entertain", the old BBC motto (as opposed to the current one which seems to be "Overpay, Overpay-off, Over produce"). That's to say a) have a point and make it b) present it in a way that results in further thoughts c) make it so interesting people want to hear more (using surprise, humour, magic, poetry, music or whatever but always with fun).

Now the children love to volunteer and so I had a group of girls sat on the stage being mini-beasts and as I talked the school listened and chuckled appropriately. Then there was a loud gasp and everyone was staring at the stage behind me – the group of girls was now minus one – but there were a pair of legs visible, sticking up in the air at odd angles. Laughter broke out. The girl had relaxed, leaned back, found the nothingness at the edge of the stage, and fallen into it. She eventually came up laughing and to this day children and teachers remind me of it. Lesson learned though – keep an eye on your volunteers!

Another assembly in another school involved my volunteers standing in front of the assembly then running to hide. There were some large plastic barrels full of sports equipment in the corner of the hall so I directed the kids to those and they hid. Moving the barrels disturbed a nest of brown gangly spiders who felt dispossessed and sought a new resting place … they scattered towards the front row of infants sat cross legged on the floor. When the screaming and crying died down I abandoned the story, finished with a prayer and assured everyone that spiders are not harmful. Not actually true though is it!? I've been bitten by several since.

That was the same school where I once did the 'Calming of the Storm' – the children re-enacted the miracle but the matching song went very badly. The idea of the ditty "With Jesus in the boat we can smile at the storm" is that we sway and then start to repeat the verse but omitting increasing numbers of words. One of the volunteers who was swaying in the boat clearly had an over-active imagination and threw up on the hall floor! As the vomit spread the cross-legged pupils moved back, shuffling on their bottoms, pushing a tide of other children backward like a slow ripple. The smell was unbelievable and a teacher who had reacted quickly came in with a mop and bucket. She began swishing the foul slop around and I again had to abandon the story, say a quick prayer and offered to sit with the disgraced child until a parent/guardian came.

Doing 3 or so assemblies a week there were far more good ones than bad but the disasters make it onto the page because they are funnier.

September was a good month all told, a recovery from some of the past, new inroads into the community and a positive approach to the future.

2. Honeymoon Over

(Or 'The Elder Strikes Back' if you want another Star Wars reference)

October was to be a busy month. Everything was up and running. The church were starting to piece together from my sermons that my theology was somewhere right of centre (evangelical but not fundamentalist, enthusiastic but not particularly charismatic) and that my politics were too. I had no idea whose cage I was rattling but the first grumbles started to appear. A church leadership team is a gang, like a gang of school kids or a gang of bikers or a ... you get my drift. There are followers and there are leaders, there are diplomats and there are bullies – each gang has them, our leadership team was no different. From one Elder I would get "well I hear the schools are going well, perhaps there's not enough time for you to preach regularly and do such good work" (translates as: your sermon was poor, concentrate on what you are good at). From another Elder, "I'm used to getting my way here. Don't do that again." (Translates as: I'm a bully, my childhood scarred me, you made me think and I don't like that as I might need to change a bit).

My wife was settling in nicely and had made friends amongst the neighbours and in church. She was singing in a local band and they were booked to perform at Christmas events already. My daughter had made friends and a steady stream came round to play, eat and ask how I did the magic tricks they saw in school. Members of the Youth Groups I ran also called on us, at all hours of the day and night. I would get calls like "I'm in a call-box, just threw up, broken glass everywhere, can you get me?" and off I'd go. We would sober them up at our house and take them home cleaned up. I make a point of not drinking alcohol so I'm available day or night.

Having said that you've got to wake me first!:

In our flat in Boscombe some years before, so my wife tells me (because I slept through it) the police knocked our door at 2:30am. Mandy went to see who it was, calling me as she went.

Two armour wearing, machinegun-toting police persons informed her that the building was surrounded and we should not attempt to leave. They were looking for flat No3 so Mandy informed them that it was the only flat with no access to the interior hallway and staircase they were now filling with troops – the door to No3 was in the car-park around the back!. Clattering commenced as the squad of police in full Kevlar kit ran back down the stairs and out into the car-park. Blue and red flashes filled the sky around our building as squad cars cut off every road in the vicinity. They battered through the door to No3 and took away the Irish chap who lived with his wife and child there – IRA apparently – who knew?!

My wife came back to bed and tried to sleep – but it was one/nil to me on that!

I had set aside Tuesday mornings for visiting people who were interested in Christian stuff, follow-up visits and Bible studies. I had a 9:30am booked with Deb, who I had met at church with her husband (who typically was not as keen as her). I found the address and knocked the door. She came to answer wrapped in a big fluffy pink towel! She said to come in and she would get dressed. I said I'd wait on the doorstep until she was dressed and she looked embarrassed, which was my intention. We did the Bible Study but I told my Minister about it and didn't go there again. There' a lot of temptation about, but you don't want to hear about the mousey/cute au-pair, the girl in the white dressing-gown or frisky old ladies. Oh! you do?

Hard luck then – try a different author – I have a normal male mind, eye and err… everything, but have remained faithful and fully intend to. So help me God.

The Shop Chaplaincy was a lovely role, everyone seemed happy when I popped in on a Wednesday afternoon – I'd spend a couple of hours wandering and chatting. I'm happy to just cheer people or listen to problems, but best of all I love the big questions (most adults are afraid to ask) like 'what about suffering', 'didn't we evolve and isn't everything just an accident', 'why did Jesus have to die?', these are the golden moments for me. Before most will talk about such things I have to earn the right. I listen. Sometimes people will chew my ear and we never get anywhere but sometimes it leads to the light!

Lesley was a shop-worker and whilst selling cuddly-toys was probably not her life-long ambition she had to accept that it was better than the farm she had left in Zimbabwe. Her husband had split and gone east to Australasia and she had arrived in Basley to stay with her daughter. She was bitter. Each time I visited her shop the result was the same, her anger poured out (Mugabe has so much to answer for: perfectly good farmland ruined to get rid of certain farmers, leaving none with the skills to use it; farm-houses trashed and burned and people fleeing with only what they can carry). This went on for weeks. Eventually I got a word in here and there, I took her back to better times in her life. I gave her a Bible and got her reading the Psalms. She felt they had been written just for her and her demeanour changed. She is now reunited with her husband and living with him in Oz somewhere, she wrote to me and said she cherishes that Bible! Joy.

Locally I was now known as 'Tim the Hymn', 'Magic Man' or 'Pastor' (the latter only used by my Afro-Caribbean brothers and sisters). The weeks passed and the contact numbers increased.

We planned a 'Light Party' to counter the Halloween festival with all its negative connotations. It was a joint-church operation (the best kind!) and every kid in town was invited. There would be food, games and stories, magic, music and all in our highly decorated parish church. We met as planning groups and much fellowship was had. One Vicar, Clive, said he'd had the offer of some balloons and would I help him pick them up? Of course, I live to help.

He picked me up next morning in his mobile air-raid shelter – a corrugated French vehicle with holes in big enough for rats (if they had no car taste whatsoever, but thankfully all the Basley rats watch Top Gear). We rattled down the country lanes to Bourne Cross Priory, where one of his monk contacts would be waiting. Parking on a downward slope, so that the car could start easily, we approached the high red brick walls that surround the Priory. There were 3 doors as far as we could see but all were locked and our knocking drew no attention. We circuited the ancient establishment again and this time found a door bell under some ivy. A troubled Irish lady answered and took us inside. I was about to ask Clive who we were meeting but he saw the movement of my lips and "Shushed" me. He indicated that I should follow and he fell in behind the house keeper who in turn fell in behind a robed monk. The procession of four completed 2 of the four sides of the quadrant and then turned sharply up some stairs. The stairs led to a windowless room in the wall which contained ladders, Zimmer frames and five huge shiny fish-shaped balloons. I saw the shock on Clive's face as the monk passed the ribbons for each balloon to us. The helium filled, hideously colourful fish bounced around the ceiling and needed reining in just to get out of the room. We processed ceremonially back around the quadrant, passing stations of the cross and statues of various saints, our ugly flying fish bobbing about totally at odds with their serene environment. Each person had one except me, at the back with two. I couldn't resist skipping for a while as a mark of unity with the rebellious fish. When we reached the exit Clive gave me two more fish to hold and he retained control of one. As we approached the tin shed that was our ride home, I feared a gust of wind might whisk me away over the trees (remember Andrew McCarthy in the 80's classic 'Mannequin'? No? Put this down and go watch it).

The challenge of course was getting the five huge fish-balloons plus ourselves into the car. We managed it by putting 3 in the back (obscuring all the windows), one under my legs and one on my lap. The car had rolled forward into a hedge while it was parked so Clive had to warm up the engine, rev hard to reverse up onto the gravel then crunch the gears and keep revving to go right, out of the car park and back into the lanes. One fish from the back bobbed about between Clive and I so with one arm I pushed it back into the rear whilst still controlling the one on my lap. Another fish then bobbed forwards and I slapped it rearwards but this time lost grip on my lap fish. I shifted to pull one away from the front windscreen but at this point my so far patient 'under leg fish' made a bid for freedom. As we drove through Basley members of the public pointed and laughed, some at the car and some at the mayhem inside.

Why did a silent order of monks have big helium-filled garish fish? I never found out. But they added to the decorations in church for our 'light party'. I ignored queries from leaders and children about the relevance of fish to All Saints/All Hallow Eve – the effort meant they were staying put!

Despite the criticism from Elders, the dramatic assemblies and the weariness that comes with hard work, October was a good month and finished with a Half-Term holiday of mostly family time.

Good ole Grandma paid our membership of the National Trust each year. Each year we vowed we would visit more of their sites, most years we managed the average of one. This was it:

We took ourselves off to London to visit a restored mansion often used in period dramas. Alice was unhappy at first but we promised nice food and she cheered up. Once in, we wandered the long corridors reading the notes supplied by NT and the signs by old pieces of furniture and suits of armour. A lovely way to spend a day, knowing that there's always lovely cake in the café at the end! We saw rooms where landed gentry had slept and the kitchens that were used in a recent Hollywood film. Alice had wandered off ahead of us – it's a rule that parents must move too slowly for children and we stuck to it despite the call of the cake.

We got talking to some very knowledgeable people who took pity on us (we were not dressed as if about to picnic at Henley) and imparted their wisdom in condescending tones. We listened and walked with them and took the lecture gracefully. We shared with them the keen interest our daughter had shown in History at school and how she was here somewhere reading up on artefacts relevant to her present school project. We shared with pride how she was bright and ahead of her age in many areas, displayed high level social skills and academic promise.

We entered a huge hushed corridor lined with statues and paintings and in the distance, coming round the corner, Alice. She stood legs apart, arms waving madly in the air and shouted into the stony silence “Look dad! Old stuff!” The echo of her voice died. Part of me did too. We apologised and moved quickly to catch her and find the café.

The end of the Half-Term found me on a ‘Men’s Weekend’ with a church. We men know what we like: a game of footie each day, a session of go-karting, action movies, a game of Risk, a rocking ‘jam’ session for the muso’s amongst us, loads of meaty spicy food and some Greco-Roman wrestling in the evening.

None of this will be happening at the men’s weekend.

We are welcomed by two men who will be taking our weekend; the tall one is dressed like Gerry out of ‘The Good Life’ and talks like him too, the shorter stocky one is like a copper from ‘The Bill’ and is wearing beige trousers, a beige shirt and a brown woollen jumper (no disbeliever, this is all true!). Let’s call him Bill. Gerry welcomed us into the lounge and explained he had a set of slides to show us of the Holy Land. Aaaaagh! Slides? Slides? (Who still looks at slides? let alone thinks they are cool?!) We looked at each-other incredulously. He proudly explained that the two projectors worked in tandem and a tape player linked to them giving a synchronised commentary..... Whoa! A TAPE PLAYER??!! Gerry was presuming that a) we hadn’t been to the Holy Land b) we wanted to hear his take on it c) we wanted to sit though SLIDES ! d) on a Friday night after a long week, any of us would be impressed by this! I woke up when he changed the circular cassette of slides – one of the men looked at me and said I could drop off for another 20min at least.

The food at Christian Conference Centres is usually cheaply sourced, over cooked and lacking in spice, flavour or real meat. The centre manager usually prefaces the meal with a welcome and the proud boast that they have staff working there from 10 different countries. The poor souls working there will be on 'pocket money' for long days of labour in areas they have no skills in, like cooking, but joined up because it was in the UK and the word 'mission' had been used. They all a) secretly want to cry b) want to spend time in London c) wonder how people can eat this junk.

The Saturday included talks from Gerry and Bill during which many of us dreamed of ways of escaping. Bill was proud of his working class background and boasted that he had no qualifications (we decided he was fishing for compliments on the basis that his self-taught knowledge and delivery skills were so good, but they weren't). Bill sold himself as a 'man's man' (as opposed to Gerry who was oblivious to his effeteness) and encouraged men to embrace 'life' (actually at this point we were all 'alive') be daredevils and challenge the norm. He actually said too many Christian men are beige and dull! When he finished his unimpressive rant I pointed out he was wearing beige. People sniggered, he didn't.

The afternoon saw us at the outdoor heated pool but Gerry came along (in Speedo's Circa 1974!) and we left. There were various reasons for the absences at the next talk. Sunday morning saw us sitting in a circle passing a ball of wool to a random man opposite – I forget why. The talk was something to do with men being afraid to sit down and just talk out problems like women do. The point seemed to be that men and women are the same and we don't need to build a shed to work together – or something like that – I know there was a shed or two in there somewhere. I was prompted by this to txt my friend Steve and offer to help him re-roof his shed.

The following discussion rejected the speaker's notion that men and women were basically the same and agreement was found around the statement that women preferred chocolate to sex. Men preferred meat or action movies. The evening fell apart as the organisers produced a DVD of Billy Elliott (a film with dancing and swearing) which was greeted with disrespect: half the men went to the pub and the other half sat and watched an action movie I had brought for just such a moment.

3. November: The Big Bang!

I've always enjoyed fire, most boys do. I have a clergy friend called David with endless stories of conflagration, most ending with "and the flames went forty feet in the air!" at which point we all cheer. Preparing for the Youth Group fireworks party was a joy then for Steve and myself (not 'shed' Steve, another one) as we bought fireworks from several sources and laid them out in his garden while it was still light. The kids arrived and tucked into pizza and crisps. Then we led them out onto the patio overlooking the now darkened garden. The first few went well and the children and leaders "ooh" and "aah" appropriately. Then came the one we couldn't identify, it looked like a small bassoon!

We hadn't known what angle to put it at nor if it should be planted in the ground or placed on a wall so we placed it loosely in the ground and lit what might have been a fuse. The children were quiet, the blackness engulfed the garden and then a rushing noise from behind some flowers and a faint glow revealed my position. I had lit the bassoon and stood well back – but it rose about 3ft in the air, hovered a moment and then angled at me. It powered toward me and I dived into some flowers and mud. To the group watching it looked like I was shot – but the firework missed me and landed with an explosion in a bush.

Steve came running with a torch – a crater now existed where the bush had been and then the torch revealed me lying on mud and scrambling to get up. The children had let out various shocked and scared noises but relief settled in when I stood up and said something corny like “that bush found a weapon of mass destruction”.

There were fireworks too from a man I visited at his home. I have leafleted a street to see if anyone responded with a request for help from the church, and as usual no-one had responded. I called on people and introduced myself but most people were out. The man that was in launched at me and I stepped back in amazement – his vitriol, his language, he took offence that I was even on his door-step. He was a hurting man but in no state to listen so I politely left.

Fireworks happen theologically too when you mention creation:

As a kid about 10yrs old I was into dinosaurs and all that usual stuff and I wanted to see how it meshed with the Biblical account of Creation. Some of it was easy e.g. “Let there be light” = a big bang. Some of it was harder e.g. the days of creation started before the orbits of the Sun and Moon giving us 24hrs had been established; I decided that ‘day’ was just ‘a period of time’. Some of the Evolutionary stuff posed more of a problem so I went to talks on the ‘Fossil Record’ and listened to lecturers like Dr Monty White, who used to accept Evolution but found the facts were against it. To this day the media and education systems largely ignore the scientific evidence that doesn’t support

Evolution though there are growing movements against it. I spoke in my new church about my confidence that 'God is the Creator' and was greeted over the next week with many complaints! One man said I shouldn't undermine school teachers by speaking against Evolution... another house group leader said I'd made life difficult for her. Other people thought I was a raving fundamentalist with my head in the sand and several said they didn't want their church getting a reputation for having my sort of theology. Some withdrew their teenagers from my group so they wouldn't be corrupted by my false teaching. I felt low. No one had come sensibly to me with a list of questions to discuss with me my standpoint or even to ask if I could accept that there are many views on this subject. I just felt ridiculed. Don't ever think that working for churches is easy.

A bright spot in the week was my evening of study in London; on this occasion the train was unusually full and I had to stand, all the way into London Bridge Station. As the many lines of track let platforms rise and thicken between them I noticed a man standing alone who had a shiny bald head and a black bushy beard. My friends who had managed to get seats were looking in other directions so I called out to them and pointed "look, there's a man with his head on upside down!" – they turned to see, as did everyone else in the carriage as the train slowly rolled to a stop. The man then looked up and saw a whole carriage full of people pointing and many were laughing, red faced and some with tears in their eyes! The man blushed and looked at his feet. I have felt guilty about this ever since, perhaps that was the last straw for the poor man and he gave up on life?! Oh how it torments me! Like when I had my first car and on a rainy day in Caerleon drove deliberately through a big puddle sending a curling wave of water over a little lady on the pavement – I hope that was not the last straw for her. I am guilty.

The knocks are not always big but they are often followed by delight: the Baptist men's curry night took the whole upper floor of the Raj Restaurant and a keen table of men discussed the menu with me as they understood that I was a regular at that and every-other curry house in the area. Just as food was served there was a crack of wood and a small bang as I hit the floor. The back of the seat and the two back legs had somehow detached from the seat of the chair I was using and once again I gazed upon the uninspiring construction of a table from underneath. I hesitantly stood and passed pieces of ex-chair to the waiter. He didn't even get me a new seat, I had to do that myself. I didn't go there again.

My daughter was doing well in school and the teachers were always glad to see me too. We would chat in the staff room or in the playground if they were on duty. Teachers would unload burdens on me and sometimes ask me to join in with lessons or assemblies where they didn't know the Christian views on a subject – so many doors were opening and my diary was getting very full but I always made it look like I had time to give – I didn't want anyone feeling I had more important things to do.

My wife was getting known in her school too and some staff came to her to talk about faith issues.

The danger when having these conversations is that attachments form and people can mistake that for other types of affection which they are currently missing. At the shops, on my Chaplaincy round, I chatted with Anna, and this happened quite invisibly. She was young and smart and had good questions, I was chirpy and fun with lots of answers. Then I said I was off to the storage/security area behind the shops and walked down the bare concrete corridor then I opened the metal concertina door of the goods lift. I walked in and pressed the light switch (which had no effect) then turned to pull the creaky door/gate closed. There in the dim light, rather too close to me, was Anna. I had no right to throw her out of the lift so had to continue closing the door and going down several floors. It became pitch black and I was aware she was moving. When we reached the destination level a little light shone in and I could even smell that she was right next to me. Never has a lift door been more firmly opened and closed! I was out, she was in. Phew!

The end of November sees the busiest season of Ministry begin – Advent! The next 4 weeks would be stack full of services and assemblies, concerts and carol singing – by the time we reach Christmas most ministers are worn out and ready to collapse. November is also a time when I try to get kids singing different songs to those usually chosen. I hate "Away in a manger" for example but teach wonderful new hymns like "Light of the World" and even golden oldies like "Shine Jesus Shine" as well as little fun ditties like "Allelu Allelu" where the kids sit and stand as they take turns to sing. Teachers tell me they sing my songs in the playground (the kids not the teachers) but mayhem ensues when the sit/stand songs kick off in the middle of lunch time in the hall!

4. December: 27 Christmases

If 27 Christmas's sounds a little excessive then let me explain: school assemblies in Advent tell the Christmas story, Sunday school does too, Christingle happens during Advent and tells the broad story from creation to redemption and then there are the Christmas plays that actually contain fractions of the real story... then just when you are exhausted the schools break up and you have the Crib Service, the Midnight service and a Christmas Day service, by which time you've said it all and just want to sleep!

Thus my poor wife and child have to put up with a dozy old grump on Christmas Day who needs a week off.

I think the worst Christmas event was when I took a Youth Group to sing carols at Gatwick airport: the teens were all excited and the big tree in "arrivals" was to be our base of operation. We had a one hour slot to fill and I had my keyboard and speaker to provide accompaniment. Despite being a reluctant member of the Les Dawson school of piano, I found most carols playable in the key of F and we launched into our repertoire with the limited gusto of teenagers afflicted by 'cool'. Suddenly one spotted a pop star, shouted their name and ran off to a far staircase, with my whole group in frenzied pursuit! I was now a lone keyboard player by a huge tree and a pile of teenager's bags and coats. I couldn't leave the gear unattended for fear of theft or security alert, yet I couldn't see the youngsters in my charge as all had now descended the staircase to see the minor celebrity!

Already tired and stressed by Christmas in general, this sent my blood pressure up, my piles down and my stomach all over the place. Good job Cromwell was wrong about it being Christmas all the time, I'd have to abscond planet earth.

Being Santa at the end of term Christmas Fair was also a disaster. I had the suit, and a cushion to stuff up my T shirt, I had a white beard and wig that would make Gandalf look like a skin-head and I was shown to my walk-in-cupboard just off the main hall which had been transformed by the school staff into Santa's Grotto. Visiting Santa was a bigger deal than I had expected and as soon as the event opened a long queue formed around the hall and down the corridor. Parents stood with excited children and the door to my little white domain opened for the first child. The boy looked at the bulky red and white clad symbol of the season before him, then stepped out into the corridor and shouted "Hey everyone, Tim Hill's in here!".

A Christmas curry night is always a welcome relief, but when the wooden chair again gave way, this time sending me sideways into the next diner, it took the shine off. So did the calls of "not again Tim, you must be doing this on purpose!" as it simply wasn't true.

Despite the overwork that comes with the season I can't help but feel sorry for various JW friends I've had over the years – they don't know what they are missing! If you don't accept that Jesus was God come to live on earth then how can you appreciate the scale of His love for us? I've found JW's to be very nice but unable to accept any teaching except from their own authorized teachers so I tend to ask them questions instead:

Me: Hi Nik, doing anything nice for Christmas?

Nik: Well although we don't celebrate Christmas like you do, we will have some parties and see family...

Me: If you saw that Jesus was God, would you celebrate then?

Nik: Well he was a god... you know, divine nature, John 1:1 and all that...

Me: yes, well your translation says "a god", all the others don't but clearly Jesus knew He was God ... didn't He say He was God?

Nik: He said He was from God

Me: Didn't He say "I and the Father are one"?

Nik: That meant their purpose was one...

Me: Didn't Thomas see the scars on the resurrected Jesus and declare "My Lord and my God!"? Who was Thomas talking to? Did Jesus say "Don't call me that Thomas"?

Nik: you know we disagree on these things Tim.

Me: yes mate, but I pray God will show you His love and you'll understand it all one day

Nik: perhaps ...how's your daughter?

Some people will talk religion, some people want to avoid it, and that makes me sad. The Chaplaincy in the shops is often an opportunity to talk deep, but it always surprises me when a potentially life changing chat can be punctuated with "That'll be four pounds fifty madam" for a moment then back to deep emotional revelation as if the customer had not ever been there!

I've always avoided strong language and have only sworn 3 times. The first was after my primary school teacher had belittled my sister in front of other pupils; I went home for lunch each day (the smell of the school dinners made me feel sick) and on that particular day I told my mum about it and called my teachers birth details into question by using the B word. My mum was so shocked she didn't tell me off! Strange. The second swear word popped out accidently in a class when I was playing word games with some Yr6's – we had to change words by one letter at a time as fast as we could; my turn came and Duck turned into F, then I carried on into Luck and Muck very quickly trying (and failing) not to blush. None of the children ever mentioned it, no one called me up on it. Strange. I still feel bad. The final swear word was that one again, this time on an acetate: the OHP was all the rage in churches for a few years as singing into a hymnbook was out of fashion and digital had not reached everyone yet. The word crept in as part of a carol, I had delegated the writing of it to my wife as I've never been a good scribe. We didn't spot the way the second and third letters of "flickering" had almost joined into one... until the Christmassy crowd stood to sing the carol what a terrible moment!

"Like a candle flame, f***ing small in the darkness..." oh my shame!

I saw the words on our church wall written large for all to read! The horror on sweet faces, oh!

I thought I would die, or be sacked, or something… but nothing came of it. Strange.

This year, as every year, something new jumped out of the Christmas narrative that I had not so far discovered. That's the joy of the season for me! I know there will be a fresh truth to find, like a jewel in the grass. This year it was about the extreme contrast of Christ's visitors: the smelly and despised shepherds compared to the fragrant and respected kings/wise-men, all should bow before Jesus.

The week after Boxing Day is time off and I try to make up for my absence by doing things my family want to do. No curry then. No board games. No action movies. No sport. I'm not really sure where those times did go, but my wife and child seemed happy.

That's the time for visiting the far away relatives too – a trip to Wales was expected. Leaving the warm decorated home my wife keeps so Christmassy and stocked, we travel down the M4 on the dark interminable slide towards the Severn Bridge, rain, wind and my father's barren house. No decorations, one comfy chair to take turns in and sparse living which carried on after rationing stopped and got worse during the strikes of the late seventies – nothing much has changed in 30yrs, except that "Last of the Summer Wine" is now watched on a large flat screen TV.

My wife and I had welsh accents as children but have lost them over the years. My daughter has never had the accent and indeed sounds quite posh even to us. The impact of this was to distance us from some of our welsh clan:

Me: (entering an uncle's house for the first time in years) Hello Pugh! How are you?

Mandy: Yes, hello uncle Pugh, good to see you!

Uncle Pugh: O, gone all posh on us av yew? Wen yew goin' then?!

And that was it.

Back home for New Year's eve, it's time to relax with musical friends, have a jam, eat large amounts of meats, breads and salady bits … and then ruin it with that stupid song everyone says they like, with the nonsense words and yet another round of an addictive chemical that comes in pretty bottles and ruins lives. Ho hum.

5. January: Back to the Future...

Just after Christmas we went back to Wales for Grandma's birthday. My wife's mother had some issues but was as warm and loving as anyone could be. She was hospitable and generous and a member of a little Chapel in the Rhondda Valley, where she had lived all her life. No, she didn't live in the Chapel, she lived in a terraced house like most other people lined up like domino's parallel with the valley sides. No not the people... the houses were lined up... oh stop it, go get a drink and come back with a less picky attitude!

She was surrounded by lovely characters, straight out of a Ruth Jones sitcom. There was a lady who turned up at your front door several times a day convinced she hadn't seen you for a long time and there was no point in telling her she was in for a cup of tea just an hour ago because she was locked into 'long lost friend' mode. It was her condition, everyone understood. Then there was Uncle Owen who, since he had discovered the internet, could not be dissuaded from printing in his study – anything you mentioned in conversation was Googled and he honestly believed people were interested in the reams of trivia he produced daily.

Then there were the names. In South Wales you mustn't giggle if you meet Rhydan Tripp or Raving Gruel, Owen Owen or Pugh Pugh. They have feelings (sorry chaps).

We had arranged for a secret gathering of the family at Grandma's favorite restaurant by the coast – she had no suspicions as we parked and walked her into the main dining area. A long table had been laid and she gave a little shriek as she saw her sisters and their husbands sat looking at menus. Then other family members came out from their hiding places and 20 of us sat down to look at menus. Ordering from a menu is more complicated than I thought previously. "Are you having the steak?", "Yes I'm thinking about having it" "oh, well I'm not sure now, maybe I'll have another thing", "well I'm sure they'll have two, we could both have it", "no, I'll settle for the pie", "why? there's chops there, you like chops", "no, I'll see what Mandy's having…" now that's just two people: each person seemed to have to discuss their order and waver about it with everyone near them. Eventually everyone had ordered, but then the drinks came: "I ordered orange juice, did you order J2O?" "No, I ordered Coke, why? Is your orange juice ok?", "Well it's not very fizzy", "Was it supposed to be fizzy?", "I just don't fancy it now, perhaps they could change it?". And so the conversation went on and on, no one quite satisfied. But someone has rightly observed "the Welsh are a people genetically predisposed to mild disappointment" – this was my family, and I love them. Anyway the meals were served and a new round of dissatisfaction began: "Oh, Gran, you've got carrots. I've got some to, but they are not very warm", "Your carrots are not warm? My carrots are not cold, but they are not very hot"… "What about you da, 'uv yew got carrots?", "No mine didn't come with carrots, but Auntie has carrots... are your carrots warm Auntie?", "What da? I can't hear you down this end of the table"... then the conversation about carrots and warmth spread down the line and reached Auntie at the other end: "Oh, that must be what da was on about... his carrots were cold", someone else piped up that da didn't have any carrots, but Gran did and hers were warm.

My wife and I were looking at each other ready to burst with laughter and tears forcing their way around our bulging eyeballs ... but we couldn't, people wouldn't understand. Instead we joined in "my carrots are not warm Gran, but they are not quite cold, they are just not hot enough..." A whole afternoon of wanting to laugh hysterically gave me a headache but it was worth it. The final straw was when Gran gave up eating saying she was too excited by the surprise. She left most of the main course, wouldn't have a sweet and on the way out to the car park mentioned that there was a nice McDonalds just down the road!!

The year lays before us and family Hill gets right to it: Alice in school and learning lots, Mandy in school and teaching lots, me in schools - also.

The term didn't start well. I called in on the first day back to find it was an inset day and the C of E Primary was still under repair after the storms at holiday time. The 'hut' classroom had been soaked and so after a thorough clean-up and a lick of paint, the carpets were replaced and the front steps had yellow edging painted on them to help children notice the danger of falling. The caretaker had just finished painting the steps and had gone to get a "wet paint" sign from his workshop. I walked in, up the steps and said "Hi" to the teacher inside. She was busy but always made time for me and said encouraging things. Like pointing out the pristine state of her classroom and how the extra funding had paid for the new .... Aaaaagh!

The caretaker appeared in the doorway with a “wet paint” sign. He looked ready to cry.

The Head teacher appeared next to him and her jaw dropped. She was about to say that someone had put footprints in the yellow warning paint on the steps, but the yellow footprints on the new classroom carpet said it all and led to ME! I looked down, I wanted the ground to swallow me! I always like to think I bring help. But I bring mayhem. Quickly I walked to the door and offered to get soap and a mop and clean the carpet, but as I did so I left a trail of yellow marks towards the door. Idiot. I should have taken my shoes off!

Every time I go near that class I get the shivers as I see those steps. I will make it up to them.

The term gets into full swing and some special events loom. Our town is having a Talent show and I’m asked to be a judge. I go to meet an old friend in Eastbourne at our favorite Oriental Buffet (you’ll never guess what happened! I had a metal chair. Part way through the meal [and I had been confident there would be no disasters as it was not wooden] the chair began to lower me towards the ground! Do you remember Bambi in the film? Walking on the frozen pond? Twig-like legs go in four directions? Yup... it’s not like I’m a Sumo wrestler or something... why me?) and I got a parking ticket, after checking with the local bobby that it was ok to park in that spot! Why me?

Another special time was a meal at the invitation of a nice lady from the Anglican Church: she had some friends she wanted me to meet and she added that they have questions for me. Oh brill! I love these willing discussions that lead to lost folk stepping towards God. I drove down the country lanes to her neat cottage with a spring in my step/car and a smile on my face.

The home was out of this world, and more out of the miniature village at Bourton–on-the-Water. I ducked to get into the narrow hall and greeted the little lady with a handshake and a warm smile then followed her into a neat lounge ducking the dark wooden roof beams as I went. She didn't need to duck, neither did her two friends who smiled and shook hands with me. We sat perched on the tiny velvet two seater settees and as we chatted I noticed the glass fronted cupboards with a collection of tiny tea cups and matching plates and below on a leather topped table a dark-wood tray containing small silver cutlery. She's a collector I noted for a later conversation.

One lady had been a Head-teacher and another was a friend of Cleo Laine, they were nice, if twee, and wanted to know what I spent my time doing. Dinner was served and we sat at a small round table properly laid but inadequate for seating even two. Our host brought out a fish meal with veg, served on those tiny plates and followed by tiny fruit pies and ideal milk. I felt the room was closing in on me, the low ceiling, the tiny leaded windows and the close proximity of 3 elderly and now quite focused widows. The one wearing the most tweed looked me in the eye and fired first: "you're very young to talk with any authority on the foundational matters of life, what can you know?!" I was taken aback.

Recovering quickly and thinking of St Paul's famous defense I launched into a summary of the religions I'd studied, the many countries I'd visited, the diverse friends of all beliefs and none who I love and share thoughts with... and so on until she broke eye-contact and seemed satisfied. The other petite pensioner now fixed a steely gaze on me and launched the torpedo that sank me… "Do the blacks have a God?"

(Stunned silence) thoughts tried to materialize like clouds trying to draw a VW beetle and failing, or like Spock's predecessor in Star Trek the Movie, like… really? That's even a question?

Where do I start? Panic mind: hit reset. Default conversation kicks in: talk about Jesus. Breathe. "Well Jesus wasn't a Caucasian... He was from the Middle East… most of His early followers were dark... some Arab, some African, He was a refugee in Egypt. He has more followers in Africa and South America than in places like Europe..." I was flailing about, wondering what I needed to explain, was this a cruel joke? Was someone filming this?

No. It was real. The nice Anglican lady saw me after church the next Sunday and said they had enjoyed it. I didn't.

Better news greeted me at the shops where the Chaplaincy had let me into the lives of very different people: One lady was Nina, an eastern European, working in a clothes shop owned by a violent Muslim trader. Things were not easy. But if he wasn't around we had good conversations and I gave her a Bible. A few weeks went by and I saw her again – she was reading the Bible and boy, it looked well read! She was eating it up and was boiling over with questions… and clearly was finding answers; I was so happy just hearing her talk and overflow with her new-found faith. She left for America with her husband after a year or so but I know she took good learning and an inner joy with her.

January was going well. Until the Talent show night.

I like to encourage people, and I knew our town had talent, so I felt confident that being a judge in this competition was going to be a good witness and I could inject humor and pace if it got a bit stodgy for the audience. Inside the little chapel the crowd was gathering, acts were registering and I took my place at the side of the stage with the two other judges, a playgroup leader and a jolly Vicar.

The crowd sat, most had come to support a relative or friend, and the compere introduced the rules and the judges. Then the first act came out; a small boy who would play piano for us... he played confidently at first, then lost his way and restarted. He then announced he could play another song better and began the second piece, but he was in error, it was worse. Now I don't think lying to people is helpful so I don't do it. If I can't say something nice I say nothing... but judges have to say something!! I said it was not very good but he should keep practicing, lift his hands, know the pieces better and keep in time. He cried.

The next act was a group of girls, about 20 of them, resplendent in matching outfits and well-spaced in the middle of the church performance area. Pounding music began and they pounced into acrobatic stances and bounced into poses... but after about 30seconds some were out of time with others and one girl sped on with the moves confidently so they all looked to her. Some of the tubby girls got out of puff after 2 minutes and one actually stopped. Others tried to copy the confident one but couldn't pull it together ... the music ended and all bowed – they beamed as if they had just won the world cup at Wembley! The other judges said well done... I couldn't. I said they relied too heavily on the one girl who knew all the moves. I said they needed to move in time and be fit enough to keep going. Some cried.

Their mums took them home, they didn't stay for the results, or even to maul me as I tried to leave. The next act might have finished them off anyway.

She was a dear old lady, you get them on talent shows sometimes, missed out on the 'Big Time' through some unfortunate contrivance and now having a last fling on stage to get noticed. The sweet pensioner bedecked in silks and smelling strongly of Lavender, swept up onto the stage and announced that she would sing her favorite hymn, the one she sang everyday while doing housework, the one that had meant so much to her for 40yrs or more.

The pianist struck up and the lady sang the first line. It was shaky and met the melody occasionally, but it wasn't great. The second line of her lifelong favorite tripped off her tongue and fell into an abyss ... she faltered and stopped. She couldn't remember the next line. People prompted her, many of us knew it! She started a line then stopped, apologized and left the stage. I wanted to laugh hysterically but might have caused offence. I cried.

I gave my honest opinion that "perhaps this is not your gift" and the other judges disowned me, apologized for my offensive remarks and ushered on the next piano abuser, a little girl who looked terrible. She was. I suggested she team up with the earlier pianist to form a comedy duo as there was a gap in the market for a "synchronized note guessing" act!

I think I upset everyone that night. A conclusion for my tired wife when I got home and she asked how it went was "our town hasn't got talent".

6. February: Joy

Leaving the wreckage of my Simon Cowell evening behind me, I strode into the second month of the year with confidence – my assemblies would be on the theme of "Joy" and I had decided to live it out for all to see.

The first Tuesday night was always a Ministry Team meeting so off I went having had a good day in school and at the after school club. The Pastor and Elders had a number of points to discuss but first wanted me to report on my work: comments had come in from the congregation that I was not very effective and perhaps I could work harder. I was floored but gave an account of a typical week. I said relationships were building, but the Team wanted to know how many people had been SAVED? I didn't know, but hoped that several had taken steps closer to God. I was told to set targets and would be reviewed again in 2 months when they wanted to see clear improvements! Humph.

Alice had brought friends from school into the youth group and Mandy had witnessed to her musical friends, could I claim those as statistics? Nope, I must get my own.

Well, I thought, at least the local non-church people appreciate what I'm doing! I love their kids and visit homes and we all have a fun time… I don't have to worry about church leaders who don't see me all week. But I do.

Wednesday Club was a cleverly named meeting for primary aged children on an evening in the middle of the week. I had some volunteers and full use of the church hall. We had started off with a handful and doubled every few months! The parents had started to stay too, they liked the lively songs, fun Bible stories, magic illustrations I thought up and we had up to 60 kids coming by February. That particular evening I had brought my "Joy" theme to WC and so we had a joke swapping session, a Bible study on Irony and the whole thing was a laugh. The parents took their children home and I was left with about 15 kids to walk back through the estate until they had all reached their homes. This was a weekly feature of our lives, like the Pied Piper I led the giggling children through the streets and we often burst into our favorite songs as we followed the paths that wound through the spaghetti shaped estate. "My God is so big, so strong and so mighty…" we all sang as the path took us under a block of flats. Emerging from this short tunnel I was struck by a thought, 'I'm suddenly all wet!' and I was. I looked up, so did the children. I was struck by a bowl and realized where the wetness had come from, so did the children. The bowl hit my face and I heard someone swear at me, and so did the children. I was more WC than Joyful.

The next WC went well as usual but on the way home I was nervous in case another incident happened. As I approached that block of flats with the tunnel I noticed smoke from the Utility Room accessed from both a door in the tunnel and the stairwell in the flats. I told the children to stop clear of the building and I went into the utility room. There was a fire! Someone had set the wheelie bins on fire! Smoke was going up the stairwell and I knew I had to act quickly: I went to the nearest house with a garden and knocked the door, a lady answered who I vaguely knew and I told her that this gaggle of children were to stand in her garden and she was to watch them like a hawk. On my mobile I was talking to the Fire Brigade. The children looked scared but I couldn't worry about that, I had residents to rescue. I ran into the front lobby and approached the first two doors, both opened and I explained that there was a fire, thus the smoke they could see, and they must get out now. They complied readily. Then I went to the next landing up and knocked and rang until everyone was aware and leaving as quickly as they could. I came down with a rather shaky lady then, as the smoke billowed from the front doors, I heard a distant siren and knew help was on its way. With no time to dither I took another deep breath and ran back into the building taking the concrete stairs two at a time and reached the top floor. I gasped fresh air at the window and knocked to the last two doors. One flat was empty, the other was occupied by a man having his dinner. I told him the situation but he closed the door on me! I rang again and he answered with a plate of food in his hand and words of non-compliance on his lips. What should I do? I lunged for his tray of keys just inside the door on a telephone table; he protested but I told him he was to come with me right then and I took him by the cardigan sleeve. We reached the bottom as the firemen were coming up the stairs and I told them everyone was out as far as I could tell. They set-to hosing down the bins and a window at the back smashed, either from the heat or from the power of the water jet.

Everyone was safe. No one said "thank you". I walked the children to their homes and apologized to parents that they were late.

Half-term in Feb is a time I use to retreat. My vocal chords were damaged years ago, in the line of work, and so I like complete silence for a few days. Everyone expects me to have something to say, but on retreat in Spain I just jog on the beach, sit on the rocks, think, eat in the café's and sleep. I come back refreshed and ready for the steep hill-climb that is the Lent season ... the approach to Holy Week and Easter... the busiest time of the year!

I know you are wondering if my gift for destroying chairs works internationally: I have to say yes as I have broken two seats on my Spanish retreats, one a metal bar stool at a Tapas Bar the other a friends patio seat. Why shouldn't it happen abroad? I often write while I'm there, see Appendix 1 for a poem, typical of the thoughts I have while gazing from my balcony over the Mediterranean. (That feisty old sea roars at the shore night and day, will it give up one day?)

Slightly tanned and feeling upbeat I finished some prep at the church and drove to the next village where I had a school booking. I didn't get there.

The country lane skirted a hill, I could see the green rising through the trees on my right and occasional traffic passed me going the other way. Then the left view opened out onto fields sloping down and away to a river perhaps a mile away. I glanced at my speedo and dials as I drove past a "30" sign and was happy that I was compliant, the sky was clearish and all was well with the world. No more cars passed the other way because a lorry was stopped, signaling and waiting to turn right, across my path. As I got close the lorry suddenly moved forward and began to take the turn straight into the front driver-side of my car!!

A lot of things happened at once: The lorry crushed the engine space of my car and my car ripped along the front of the lorry with a shrieking grind, my car kept moving and the lorry kept coming… I thought "I can't die now, Alice is about to do exams and this will upset her and ruin her schooling" I looked towards the edge of the golf course and then right at the cars behind the lorry… I couldn't die now, I'd seen the impact that witnessing a fatal car crash had had on a lady in a church I'd worked for, it broke her mind and I was not about to do that to anyone! I thought of Mandy who was currently home ill, I wondered if my car would stop or topple over the curb and roll down the bank onto the Golf Course to the left of me… I wondered if this would be my first hole in one (yes, I did think that!)... I became aware of fire. I had been holding the steering wheel in a fairly good position and in the split second of impact I wisely bent my elbows, and so my arms did not shatter, I relaxed and absorbed the shock. The airbag had not gone off (I'm told it needed to be a hit on the front for that to happen) and I must have hit the steering wheel hard with my body, but it was my hand that was on fire. Glass was flying like a shower of diamonds and then, in a moment, the slow motion effect caused by so many thoughts at one time just phased into real time.

There was noise, horrified faces, skidding as my car came to rest at the curb. In the mirror I could see behind me the damaged lorry and I wondered how the driver was? Had he lost concentration for a moment? Was he on his phone while waiting to take that turn?

A thick hairy hand appeared on my left shoulder, a small man jumped into the front passenger seat and started talking rhythmically checking things, stating things, phoning the emergency services, using code words. He said he'd been a fireman for 15yrs and would sort me out. The big hand resting lightly on my shoulder had a voice, I couldn't see the owner of it as I was trapped in the forward position by the dashboard which clamped my legs, the steering wheel close to my chest and a pain that stopped me moving. The voice was gruff and thick like the hand, it said "It's all right, we'll look after you, the police are on their way with others, I'm going to pray for you. You are Tim Hill right? I met you on a children's camp once... Dear Heavenly Father..." I was starting to tingle. I didn't want to lose consciousness, people might freak if it looked like I was dead.

Pain in my chest. Glass in my clothes. Brightness outside. My hand still on fire, but no flames or even smoke. Sirens. Police I think, one near my car talking into a radio, one putting out warning signs and talking to the queue of drivers stuck now, probably for a long time. Sorry.

The first ambulance arrived, but it was on the way to be serviced and had no useful gear inside, it soon left. Fire service teams – I heard a man say "What?! He's still alive? In that mess?!" I breathed slowly and deeply, control, stay in control!

I prayed silently: Lord I know I'll meet you one day but don't let this be it please!

The second ambulance arrived, but it was a Volvo estate vehicle and could only help a bit, they did feed a neck brace into the car and secure my head position. A grinding noise again, but not random and evil, more controlled and close. The firemen were cutting the top off my car as the doors were bucked and useless. Suddenly more light and air, the top was off, I'd never really wanted a convertible I thought, but it was out of my hands.

A third ambulance arrived as the row of cars reversed, turned and left the lane deserted but for the teams working on my area of chaos. It was an air ambulance and the Golf Club manager was protesting because they had landed on a nice green. They came over, asked if I was expected to live, received a positive reply, and flew off.

Dizzy but talking now, I started to ask questions, then gave up, it was too tiring and I was in pain. When the fourth ambulance came it was welcomed by all! It was a full sized fully equipped emergency unit with a male and female who quickly got a stretcher and, with help from the firemen, lifted me out of the wreckage and onto the board. They strapped down my body, arms, legs and head, carried me flat to the ambulance and heaved me in. They clicked the stretcher into the on-board bed and told me not to move! I splurted a laugh "MOVE???" I said trying not to sound ungrateful. I couldn't move a muscle!

The nice lady asked me my name and took out a huge pair of scissors! She began cutting off my clothes! Eek! My new black trousers and a favorite shirt, shredded! This was weird.

I was feeling the cold. She was feeling my body. My personal belongings from pockets were being fished out, noted and put in a plastic bag – the male para-medic was helping with this.

They stopped when they found a pink plastic finger, they thought it was something kinky... I assured them I was a magician and that was part of a trick. The bag of belongings was sealed, stowed (and later lost by the hospital) and the doors were closed. They asked me which hospital I would like to go to as we were equidistant between two. I knew the one near where I lived was awful (many mistakes made with my family and others I knew) but the other hospital was nowhere near my town and would make it inconvenient for visitors. So I chose the bad but closer hospital. Mistake.

"How bad is the pain Mr Hill?" she asked.

"On a scale of what?" I asked

We took a roundabout at speed and the sirens sounded to warn drivers who don't look in their mirrors.

"How much pain and where is it?!"

"Well if death is 10 and childbirth is a 9, and I'm obviously in the dark on those, I'd guess my hand is an 8 my chest is a 6 and my legs are a 4"

She gently brushed tiny shards of glass off my skin and told me I was not cut or bleeding and in that sense was lucky.

We took two roundabouts, leaning heavily, not slowing and I guessed where we were. I was right. Why is everything a competition? I hate that about me.

My wife had been phoned and she told prayerful friends like Pam, Ray and Jill. Mandy was at home but the friends got to the hospital before I did and as I was trolleyed from the ambulance to the Emergency room I heard Pam, Jill and Ray "there he is", "Yes, that's him" "let's follow him!"

People slid me onto a hospital trolley/bed and drove me down a corridor, Pam Ray and Jill in hot pursuit … crashing through heavy wooden doors I sharply swung into an examination area. There was beeping and my head swam, thoughts merging with the white walls and the smell of medical chemicals. A huge black male nurse appeared by my side and spoke comforting words. A vision of beauty appeared on my right side and busied herself before starting another body examination. Her skin was so smooth and golden that it didn't exist in chemical form, it was more ethereal, like a shimmering projection of gold on a gentle cloud of vapor. I looked at the male nurse, back at the gorgeous doctor, then at him again.. "Is it me or is she… WOW!?" He coughed politely and looked me in the eye, “You’re ok mate!” I lay there and watched her work.

She decided my sternum was broken and dispatched me to x-ray. As I sped on my trolley bed we entered a public area and I heard 3 distant voices “there he is!”, “let’s follow him” “Tim are you ok? ...” they faded into the distance and I faded too, wanting to sleep but the pain in my hand was furious and hot.

They x-rayed my sternum and concluded that if it had broken inward then I’d be dead. As it happens the break was outward so no vital organs were punctured but I had to remain still so it could heal ... weeks of stillness... I’m not good at ‘still’.

The X-rays of my hand (which they later lost) showed broken bones and distorted muscles – seems the shock of the impact found a home in my left paw. It was unusable for weeks.

The big black medic took me back to the ER then waited with me as the admin people decided where to send me. He had some relationship issues and needed to find God fast. I gave him some advice Jesus left us about love, and said I’d spend some time with him when I was better.

At last a space was found for me on a ward and they wheeled me out to the lift – “there he is” “we’ve been praying for you” “how are you feeling” I’d forgotten about my little entourage! They scuttled behind my trolley-bed. Wonderful friends, comical corridor antics! I owe them, and the retired fireman and his mate with the big hairy hand. The whole thing could have been lonely and lacking in humor, devoid of spirituality and utterly depressing. It wasn’t. It wasn’t great though.

The ward was full once I was slotted into place. Next to me was a man in mental turmoil: he would press his buzzer for attention and when the nurses came he would attack them. When they left him alone he would start pulling the tubes out of his arm and side, spraying smelly fluid all over the floor, he would take a few steps then collapse. When staff came and lifted him back into bed he would attack them. It was horrible to watch and I wanted to help him. The pain was that I couldn't get involved, I grew sad and frustrated. The next day the cycle of violence continued and I had to ask the staff to pull a curtain around my bed as I couldn't bear to watch. Couldn't they sedate him? Wasn't there a secure unit?

The communications were flying about invisible to me and soon people started turning up to visit. Thankfully some brought tasty snacks and bananas as the hospital food was bland, over boiled and portions were minute. Clergy friends rocked up at all hours as they don't have to abide by visiting times, at one point there were 3 Rectors, 2 Vicars 2 Chaplains and an International Evangelist I didn't even know! They sat around my bed, introducing each other and saying what work I had done with them. They all bowed in prayer and in a moment of silence I heard a nurse outside say to the Sister on Duty "oo's e then? Bleedin' Archbishop of Canterbury?"

I chuckled inwardly, and wondered if I should tell her I actually knew the Archbishop, but thought better of it.

Night time on the ward was depressing, the pain kept me awake even though they had finally found me some pain-killers. The disturbed man next to me was asleep but the young guy opposite, who had just had his appendix removed, was in a lot of pain. He called out for a while but nobody came. In the dim light I heard him crying and I could do nothing. He pressed his buzzer. Nothing. I pressed my buzzer. Silence! Where were all the staff? It was the wee small hours, but he needed more than a wee… so he staggered out of bed, gripped his mobile drip-stand and headed shakily for the toilet. He didn't make it. He got to the door of our ward, slid to the ground still crying with pain, and tried to crawl to the WC. He didn't make it in time and the humiliation for this man was overwhelming. I heard him calling out to a member of staff, a male nurse had appeared and I thought things would now improve.

"Oh! You silly boy, you've poo'd yourself. Why did you do that then? We are not doing this in England, now I am being the cleaner eh?"

The guy sobbed "Well I called and I buzzed, if you were doing your job this wouldn't have happened!"

The nurse bit back "Who are you to tell me my f***ing job eh, sonny? You are making the mess. There are no cleaners until 9 of the morning. You are smelly. It is disgraceful."

The young guy swore at the nurse and eventually staggered back to his bed and slept. I didn't. It was all too much.

Day 2 in the hospital was not much better. Several of the nurses had poor English and I couldn't understand them, but they were only offering terrible food anyway. One nurse did look professional, the care she showed gave me hope and she treated each of us like actual people not unwanted intrusions... well done Helen from Guildford!

I was to have tests today but first the Doctors flocked around the beds and I got some attention because of my injuries. The lead medic took my pulse and blood pressure then looked disturbed and ordered a crash cart and pulled the curtain back around my bed, excluding the junior doctors. I heard a kerfuffle and some nurses came. I asked what was going on and was told my statistics were very low and a team was coming! I asked the Doctor if he had read my file? Did he notice that my stats are always very low? He went quiet, read the file and cancelled the emergency. Like my dad I have a very slow heart.

The time came for me to be wheeled downstairs for tests. I could hear a nurse talking on the phone, asking around for a porter to take me downstairs. No one was available, apparently there were only two on duty today in the whole hospital!

I didn't want to miss the tests so I suggested to a passing nurse that perhaps someone else could wheel me down, I offered to do it myself but she said I must remain flat and still.

Eventually a cheerful chappie came along, unlocked the wheels on my bed and rolled me down the corridor. We used the large lift to go down and then he asked me where I was going. I told him I hadn't been informed but thought he had been. He parked me outside some rooms next to an insipid painting of a horrible pink flower in a sickly orange vase, and went inside. He came out and said this was the right place and the specialist would be out soon. He had to go and collect someone else upstairs somewhere. Well best of luck to them!

I don't remember what the test was but it was only the first of three that morning. Trouble is there was no joined-up thinking going on. After the first test I was pushed outside again to once again admire the horrible pink flower in the sickly orange vase. Art therapy it was not! After a long while of just lying there I asked a passing nurse what was happening and she went into one of the rooms to find out. Returning she informed me that a Porter was being sought, to take me back upstairs to my ward, but no-one was available at the moment. The specialist came out at this point and explained that they needed the Porter would need to have enough time to take me up, wait, then bring me back down for the next test. I asked where the next test was to take place and was told “that room there” as fingers pointed to the door at the other end of my bed. I apologized for questioning the system but suggested that why then couldn’t they just not get a Porter, but instead take me into the next room for the next test. It was like a revelation to them! I just thought it was blinking obvious. Telling me how clever I was, they took me into the next room and introduced me to an academic looking lady in lab coat, glasses and power clothes. Some kind of genius perhaps?

The room was barely big enough for my trolley-bed and she had some difficulty moving around it to get to various bits of machinery on workbenches around the periphery of the inadequate area. She squeezed by me to switch on a strange looking box, a plastic grey unit that would have looked at home in Patrick Troughton’s Tardis! It had an arm that came out and a flexible bit on the end and a wire going to some sort of dot-matrix printer. The lady helpfully confessed that she hadn’t used this machine for some time and that then it didn’t work well. She switched it off and on again but,,, nothing. I could see the power lead hanging down but I didn’t want to seem cocky. She asked me about my injuries then said she would ring for a technician to see if they could get the machine working, but it may just be a bit old. I gently suggested she plug it in. She didn’t seem at all embarrassed! She had it working in no time and it began making some rusty grating noises. Then the printer part of it sprang to life, and she moved the arm part over my chest and hand. Then she sat on her stool, put her head in her hands and reached a tissue out of her large leather handbag. It was a petulant machine she told me, something always interfered with the signals so it failed to print out its findings. Unbelievable! Having survived terrible nursing, incompetent doctors, almost extinct porters and a patient movement system that was less efficient than the railways, I was now stuck with a machine that had tantrums and a lady unwilling to fight it! I was more fascinated that angered, the more I thought about my predicament the more I understood why society is in a mess. Outdated machines, systems that are ill-conceived and inflexible and not enough staff.

She rang someone and they talked about the machine. She went all along the worktops switching things off and unplugging them, I pointed out her mobile phone was on and that signs all over the area suggested phones must be switched off as they could interfere with machines. She switched it off and didn't seem to mind that I was talking her through this situation as if I worked there. I wondered if she was on three times my salary or four?

Someone came in and advised her to switch the machine off at the plug as it had an internal battery it could run on for a while, and the external power lead was what muddied the signal to the printer rendering it useless. They were right, the machine had been interfering with itself! Now tamed, the little beast clattered and buzzed happily, printing a picture of a broken thing. My sternum apparently. She thanked me for all my help and patience and rang for a porter to take me off for my third test. The same chappie came along and collected me, took me for the test then into the big lift and parked me back in the ward with the crazy guy busy attacking some nurses and the young chap who was sleeping off his terrible night in the toilet.

My visitors that afternoon were kind and smuggled more spicy food in for me. That night I had the curtain drawn round again and evening visitors had to step inside as if visiting a fortune teller at a fair-ground.

Day 3 began with someone in uniform rousing me at 7am to ask if I was awake. She asked if she could get something for me - I asked for more sleep, but she said it was time to work. I pointed out that I couldn't. Perhaps she didn't understand the concept at play here. The gaggle of Doctors flocked around the bed as yesterday, a different guy leading them this time. He took my pulse and blood pressure and dropped the file he was carrying onto my bed. He sent a young understudy to fetch the senior nurse quickly. I asked what the problem was and he said my readings were very low and I needed immediate attention. "Read the file" I said with exasperation. He read the file.

Later that morning the doctor assigned to my case came to see me. He asked what he could do to help me. I said perhaps a secure unit for my neighbor, and apology from the male nurse who berated the poor appendix guy, some systems that worked, some new machines that didn't interfere with themselves... and he could let me go home. He said I was not fit to go home, I had to stay here and recover. I said there was no way I could recover in this chaos and it was stressing me out. He reluctantly signed me off so that I could go home. It was then the loss of my personal belongings was brought to light, and that my file had been set up in two different spellings of my name. That's understandable as welsh names like Tim Hill are notoriously complicated. Each of my files were incomplete (and one of them had mistakenly been sent to Crawley hospital!) and my x-rays would have to be re-done as they had got lost!

A clergy friend, Pete, took me home and laid me in my bed where I spent several weeks, on my back, in peace. Mandy was recovering, Alice was just fun, and work suggested I take the full 3 months to recover. But I didn't, there were souls to save!

Pete and his wife, like several other ministers, were wonderful during those long days, I miss Pete since his early departure, a good friend gone, at peace, bless'im.

The little close in which we live is a happy Neighborhood, I started a Neighborhood Watch there and ran it from our home, but the folks are so lovely it's really a joy to do. They were kindness itself during my recovery and not because there was one less car parking in the few spaces we have, though that was a noticeable fact. February turned into March and that slipped by into April so doesn't get its own Chapter (no don't feel sorry for March, if it's that sad go write a book about your March! Mine was dull, like daytime TV used to be. No, March! You'll get no sympathy from me.)

7. April: Resurrection and Joy!

Cautiously back on my feet, I was fed up of having ideas and not being able to act on them. My left hand was back into shape and I went and bought a car, I had to get driving again though I was nervous at first. I needed to go to my friend's 40th Birthday party in Brixton so that motivated me and I even wrote him a song! Adolfus was a lovely man and the invitation said I only needed to bring myself so I didn't take food, or a present. Arriving early at the red brick chapel I parked neatly and strolled into the hall. Only the caterers were there. An hour after the party started I had got to know the caterers pretty well. This was an all-black community and lateness was the norm, but I didn't know that, or what I was eating, but the caterers were glad of someone to fuss over! Two hours after the start time the revelers started to roll in and many of them had brought food! Didn't anyone read invitations?

I love spicy chicken – and that's what they brought, all 200 of them, enough to feed London! And the keyboard arrived, then the host and birthday boy arrived. He was seated at the top table and his family sat around him like body guards, but he had seen me, I know because he winked. People stood to make speeches about him and some read poems, finally after being in that hall for 4hrs I was asked to sing my song. This white boy walked to the keyboard, switched on the mic and sang. From the first line in I noticed people starting to talk to each other. Then everyone was talking, including the birthday boy! No one was listening, in fact by verse 2 I couldn't hear myself for the noise. It was rude. I sat down. No one clapped or even spoke to me. My bubble was burst.

More food was brought out, well spicy chicken anyway, and a young guy approached the keyboard. Best of luck with that I thought and took another drumstick. The kid could play but his singing was all over the place, he warbled and took 12 notes to sing "J-E-S-U-S" and he did it over and over... it really had no melody and made no sense as he wailed out word after word stretched over many random notes. Then he stopped. Everyone stood and applauded! I stood, and went home.

That wasn't the only big birthday. Another good friend in Wales, Nigel, was reaching a grand age and he had phoned me months before to check that Mandy and I could make the date. He said it was to be in a very posh Chinese restaurant in the new Cardiff Bay area. He specifically asked me to be serious and not fool about or do anything silly. Me?!

I dressed smartly and Mandy approved my clothes first. We got to Wales in plenty of time and picked Nigel and his wife up – he asked if we could all go in my car as it was a seven seater and much newer than his. We all looked and smelled great as we got to Cardiff and found our way to the restaurant. It was very nice indeed with indoor waterfalls and all the staff dressed in golden silk pajamas. I was on my best behavior and he noticed, thanking me before discussing the menu. There were guests from all over

South Wales and the West Country, all sat around big circular tables making polite conversation. We ordered food and I washed my hands (I always do before I eat) then squeezed back into my seat which was rather too near a long wall. I sat and smiled, then frowned and looked down at the plate in front of my face... the back legs of my chair disintegrated and the table came up to meet me. No! I was going down! I was now sat on the carpet with my hair level with the table. A few little screams and gasps and then laughter, spreading like smoke through the whole huge room... I held up a piece of wood and feebly said "Sorry mate". More laughter. But he wasn't joining in, oh dear. The petite manager of the restaurant came over and apologized over and over. He gave me a deep bow, I gave him some pieces of chair. They brought me a new chair but there wasn't room to get it into my little space by the wall, we had to move the whole table causing everyone to stand, I gave them bits of wood. I like giving people things.

On the way home my car broke-down and we had to get picked up by the AA on the motorway. My friends other guests had gone on ahead to his house, but his mum, who was babysitting, wouldn't let them in because she didn't know them and she was protecting the children! They went home, we got there late and also went home. Strange night.

We were still in Wales having our Easter 'break' when Gran had her colostomy bag put in. It was shared as news around the neighborhood in much the same way other communities might talk about a neighbor having a new boiler put in or a block paved drive. We arrived in the little terraced miner's house with the tiny rooms and the low ceiling to find gran grappling with a dilemma. She did this by ringing everybody she knew. Her address book on the tiny hall-table was completely blank except for the pages labelled H and M: those pages were completely full.

H stood for Home – so she had listed everyone in no particular order.

M stood for Mobile so she had listed all her contacts who had mobile phones.

Her particular dilemma this day was around the carrying of the colostomy bag: should she have it in a shoulder bag or would that be too high? Should she have it in a handbag or shopping bag, or would that be too low? She sent me to the under-stairs storage area where she kept the fizzy pop and some Betaware products from the 60's. She asked me to bring out some bags and we tried them one by one, the colostomy bag with its warm liquid contents sloshing about was lowered by the rubber tubes into each bag and none seemed right. Tesco's, Sainsbury's, Lidl and a flowery beach bag – nothing was saying "trendy body-fluid concealer" today. One said "Bag For Life", surely that was a winner?! The morning wore on and we scoured the bottom of forgotten cupboards and wardrobes without finding the holy grail – then a neighbor came to the door: "I eared at the Pharmacy that you's looking for a bag for to put yor colostomy bag in, so I brought this…" he held forward a straw woven ladies shoulder bag with a flower motif and long handles. Gran felt it was a lovely gesture but not quite right – then as he was leaving a friend turned up who had been at a prayer meeting and someone had prayed that Gran would find the right bag to carry her colostomy bag in. The friend had rifled through her collection of bags at home and had brought over several to try.

The phone started ringing at about mid-day and mostly it was people with suggestions about what kind of bag was most suitable but some just wanted to find out if a bag had been chosen yet... some called every hour that afternoon. We had lunch and then resumed the quest. More people came, their relatives came, friends of the relatives came, relatives of the friends of rel... you get the idea...

By evening Gran had settled on a leopard print shoulder-bag that she modelled jauntily up and down the living-room with a sparkle in her eye. Nothing says sexy like a leopard print colostomy bag holder.

No chairs lost their structural integrity during that visit to Wales as far as I can remember - it seems not every restaurant has disintegrating chairs. We went to a nice Chinese near Basley with friends who work at a local airport, a civilized evening out I think my wife said.

Unfortunately the waiter who had taken our drinks order managed to tip the whole tray load over my left side! Jacket, shirt and trousers soaked! “Oh! So solly for de allwet!” he apologized. My wife didn’t know whether to laugh or cry so did both. I retreated to the toilets and set about drying my jacket under the hand-dryer. Then I took my shirt off and dried that, it was stained and sticky. Then my trousers but of course I wasn’t about to take them off, just keep them under the dryer, but it was too high on the wall to affect them much so I tried, in my half naked state, to jump close to the hot-air spout. That didn’t work so I put my shirt on and undid my trousers, a man entered and I sheepishly offered “Drink spill” but he just snorted and went into a cubicle. White shirt swishing about and hopping wildly to get my left leg close to the drier I lost balance and fell towards the sinks and the window area behind them. My right arm came round and saved me from falling but I slumped over the sinks and gasped with annoyance. At that point the chap came out of the cubicle, glanced at the sinks, and me draped over them, and left the facilities. I tidied myself as best I could and went back to our table.

"Oh! So solly for the all wet" the manager kept repeating and was only satisfied when we accepted free food on him. Clearly the drinks were on me.

The church were glad to see me back in action but most did not know about the magic tricks I had been learning before the accident. I had noticed that children remember tricks and tell their parents when they get home, so I thought I would learn some more for school assemblies – and the occasional Family Service. However the first time I illustrated a Family Service talk about improving our lives by cutting out certain bad behaviors, by chopping off my arm with a big guillotine, I found out that Christian audiences are squeamish! As the blade came down most people covered their eyes and several children had to be carried out crying. The Vicar didn't see any of this as he had put his hands in front of his face and turned away from me. Strange.

Tricks can have unwanted effects: In a school assembly where I was talking about being set free from sin, I pulled out a pair of hand-cuffs. The boys all sit up immediately as the shiny steel restraints linked by thick steel chain glistened and clanked, and each hoped they could have a go at escaping from them. Of course being "child safety" aware I instead looked to the row of teachers at the side of the hall for an assistant. A lady teacher I didn't know volunteered and walked to the front. I took her hands and told her this wouldn't hurt, to which she said nothing but gave a small inappropriate giggle. The large school hall went hush and children strained to see Miss trying to get out of the cuffs. She then turned to me, cheeks red and eyes large and offered her hands, palm up, towards me. She was glistening with sweat and stifling a giggle, her legs started to do a little on the spot running movement and her mouth opened slightly but had nothing to say, well nothing for an audience of children anyway. I suddenly realized what was happening, removed the cuffs and sent her back to her seat in a state of blushes and embarrassment.

Ladies are a mystery to me. None more so than a dear elderly woman with a name something like Bellanastasis Lyon. She lives in my Parish and the Vicar took me the first time I went to see her. The house was a rather dated bungalow and it felt crowded as we entered because, although she lived alone, the hallway was lined in old tapestries depicting knights and nobles in armor and attendants serving them. Sitting in the lounge I noticed two identical silver pots dominating the fireplace and a display cabinet to the right full of willow pattern plates and other oriental looking artworks. We stayed and chatted and I found her delightful, what's more she was clearly interested in the Christian faith.

I returned within weeks and this time found the moment to ask about the artefacts in the house. She gave a short history of each and I was enthralled. There was a knock at the back door and she excused herself to attend to the grocery boy who always came to the kitchen door and whom she paid in pennies! While she was out the back I tipped one of the large silver pots which stood sentinel to the fireplace and saw what I hoped for – a hallmark. Matching silver pots – I had seen a single one like it on TV and that had been valued at £30,000 ! A perfect pair would be astronomically valuable. I asked her about the cream colored chaise-lounge she was sat on as I had seen one in a photograph on TV recently.

She stood and reached for a photograph album then invited me to sit with her on the intriguing ivory seat. The bejeweled album cover opened to reveal old sepia snapshots of elegant Victorians. She showed me the page with a photo of the chaise-lounge, with 4 girls in pretty lace dresses sat on it and two dignified adults stood behind – it was the same picture I had seen on the TV – in a documentary about the Romanov family! I was sat on the same setee... the one Anastasia and her sisters sat on... it was hard to take in.

“So these ornaments?” I began to say... but she finished my sentence, “come from the palace in St Petersburg”. I was dumbfounded. Looking down and trying to get a handle on the situation, I observed another family gathering... “so that family, called Bowes-Lyon..?” the lady looked at me with a little sparkle in her eye like a tiny diamond that had hoped to be discovered for centuries and had finally caught some sunlight, “yes, my cousins, that little girl is the Queen Mother”. I sat back and drew a deep breath. Wonderful.

I advised her that day that she should get better locks on her windows and doors. I suggested the tapestries would be of great interest to the National Trust and that she should insure many of the items in the home specifically.

I only saw her at home once more and she told me with excitement and some surprise that the National Trust had sent some experts down and that many of her things were to be put on display in a huge mansion in the Midlands. The tapestries were going to be restored and hung in a great hall somewhere and whilst they were still hers, the nation would look after them. She was evasive about how exactly she inherited them or why she didn’t have royal connections anymore. She had left Russia as a little girl and had been re-united with these treasures at some later time, almost all trace of her Russian accent was gone and I got the feeling there was so much more to learn but her anonymity was a safety blanket. I wondered if she was Anastasia.

8. May: Am I Funny or Strange?

My church leaders were happier with my progress as they saw it. Compliments had come in from several schools and from their own children and grand-children so life was a little easier for me and for us as a family. People often said I was funny and should be a comedian. I knew that one didn't automatically follow the other but nevertheless thought I'd give it a go. I did a couple of 5minute slots at gigs in Worthing and Birmingham and found the same skills employed in preaching could be used to good effect in comedy. I was confident in-front of a crowd so that was half the battle, I always found something to say so there were no awkward silences, and I could talk about current affairs from a reasonably informed point of view, throw into the mix the odd funny poem and a magic trick or two and there I was: a reasonable entertainer, but not a great stand-up.

Whenever I did magic someone would come and tell me that as I was a Christian I shouldn't be doing magic – usually it was a lady of a certain age and always they presumed they were the first to tell me and that I would stop. I wanted to tell them to "go get a life" but restrained myself and explained the use of "illustrations" to make a point memorable and the lack of anything sinister in my tricks.

Like the Easter story with levitation – that year 11 lad will never forget being my volunteer: I told the mixed assembly of teenagers how Jesus was laid in a tomb and rose up – I got him to lay on a plank balanced on two chairs, then I took one chair away! Camera phones popped out all over the hall… I continued to tell how Jesus came alive again, taking away the plank the boy was lying on… gasps of "cool!" and "no way!". I always pass a hoop around the volunteer to show there is no support – then I replace the plank, replace the chair, remove the blanket I had laid on his body, and asked him to stand!

As this goes on I talk about the surprise of the soldiers and later the disciples – they couldn't take in what they were seeing! Perhaps Yr11 couldn't either.

Growing in confidence in front of comedy crowds I engaged professional comedians for shows in local theatres and halls. The term "Clean Comedy" became a problem for many people: Christians told me that comedy was rude and they wouldn't come, whereas regular comedy fans told me they wouldn't find it very funny as clean comedy wasn't very good. I would ask both types of people if they had ever been to a clean comedy gig and all said that they hadn't! It was an up-hill struggle but those who came had a good time… except for one village in Sussex where it went down-hill like Eddie the Eagle… off at speed and certain to crash-out. The venue was a school hall and the crowd of over a hundred seemed up for a good night. Over half were locals from the village including about 30 from a very good church I had links with. I introduced the first act after a bit of banter and magic, but it was like throwing the nice gangly young comic to the lions. Silent lions. A few folk from out of town did laugh and join in the banter, but the atmosphere was like the freezing waters that took down the Titanic. The Green Room set aside for the acts was a home economics class-room and at the half-time break I went in to talk to the lads – only to find them fighting over who could put their head in an oven first! Neither wanted to go out and do the second half! The crowd didn't like me much either but my daughter Alice, who had assisted me during a few tricks, had gone down well. Perhaps she would do the second half?

At the end I was swamped with complaints and people asked for their money back. I told them I had paid the lads from Manchester but would give refunds out of my own pocket.

"But why weren't they funny?" asked an angry Elder, "they were" I replied, "in the other venues people laughed, you just didn't get it, the audience didn't understand the comedy".

He explained to me that his people did understand comedy, they found Morecombe and Wise funny, they always found Elder Smiths 'English man, Irish man and Scotsman' joke extremely funny… my comedy night just wasn't funny. None of my friends will play there again.

Back in normal society my youth groups were growing and I picked snippets from conversations that indicated inexperience in the wider world. Of course it was my job to widen their cultural horizons so I borrowed the local school mini-bus and took them to South London. My little group of 10 were all white and, although there was a Chinese family in our town, my suspicions about their lack of international experience were soon confirmed. We went up the A23 into Coulsdon, "oh look there's 2 black men!" said an excited spotty boy. We progressed to Purley where several Ghanaian ladies in wonderful colorful dresses with matching hats were strolling down the high street. "Oh look at what they are wearing! I'd be embarrassed to wear that" said one of the girls in the back. The bus trundled on into Croydon. The evening street scene was vibrant the colors and smells of Jamaica, Ghana, Nigeria, Ceylon and more wrapped our little vehicle in a bubble of tasty joy. "There's some more black men, and more over there, and... where are the white people?" The spotty lad and his friends were now mesmerized, "is this a black-man convention?" they asked naively.

I took them for kebabs and on the way home explained that diverse populations were normal and our town was not. In fact our youth group was not. In fact the BBC had turned up to shoot a piece about school life in one of our local educational establishments only to find there was one black face in the entire building. They packed up their equipment immediately and left having done nothing.

In schools I often teach a series of lessons called Bible Explorer: five one hour sessions that take the class through either the New or the Old Testament. The Yr5 or 6 children enjoy the storytelling and the classroom is turned into a map to help them with the geography of it all. It works on a number of levels and even the most easily distractible children can cope with it. What joy for me then when after lesson 2 of the Old Testament, 2 of the more boisterous boys approached me to say that they didn't used to believe in God, but they did now! All I do is tell the Bible stories, God speaks for Himself!

Half-Term at the end of May is an opportunity to go camping. I wouldn't take it – camping is awful. The central idea is that you leave comfort behind and pay money to be deprived. Then you have to pretend it is fun. I visited some kids I knew, who were on a Christian camp based at the boggy end of a racecourse. I smiled as they told me of muddy exploits and meals that went wrong, then I went home via a local curry house.

For several years I've helped with the "churches team" at a huge regional show. Tens of thousands of visitors wander through fields given over to stall-holders selling everything from Tractors to tin openers, Pigs to life insurance. Being a Chaplain means meeting people from all walks of life and listening – one minute I'm hearing from a whiskery farmer about his sick cow, the next I'm meeting Penelope Keith! And whilst I've never been a fashion guru, I do know a good purchase when I see one: the black leather cowboy hat, the Bavarian green corduroy jacket, oh yes! I got reductions on those bad boys and took them home with pride! Of course my wife and daughter were appalled and I'm not supposed to wear them (but I do occasionally when they are not around!}.

With Gran ill it was off up the M4 for me and back to the 1970's, err, I mean the Rhondda. The people are lovely and welcoming and always have somewhere to put your umbrella, raincoat and boots. As I drove through the grey streets lined with identical houses I reminded myself that each one contained 3 generations of beautiful family, love and joy and a 50" flat screen TV that everybody watched all day.

Arriving at Gran's it was clear things were moving on quickly: There were uncles and aunts upstairs and down: I love them all but we could hardly move let alone get furniture down the tiny steep staircase with the wood chip wallpaper and 3 birds nailed to the wall at head height.

The idea was that because she was ill, her front room would become her bedroom. So a bed and bedside cabinet were to be brought down; but by who? The main contenders were all pensioners so I stepped in and volunteered to take the weight of the bed. We got it round the bedroom door but despite it being a small frame bed we couldn't take the top corner of the stairs. I suggested I stand down some stairs and they pass it over the balustrade and I would take the weight then pass it to people at the bottom of the stairs. Over the top it came and I braced myself with my back against the wood-chip and one hand on the wooden rail that traversed the length of the staircase. The whole rail and its fixings came off in my hand. The bed now at my shoulders and the rail hanging limply I noticed black dust, coal dust falling out of the holes where the rail had been screwed to the wall.

Eventually the bed and a small bedside table were manhandled into the front room area. Then the debate began: "She don't wanna sleep with her ed under the curtains do she?!" said one, "well she's not going to like having 'er ed by the door either!" offered another. "Let's put her on the other side of the room by the fireplace", "but that means moving all the furniture around, the chairs and the big table and the phone…", "well let's give it a go and see how it looks is it?".

They did. It looked all wrong. "But if you av it this way she'll have to bend over her bad side to reach anything on the bedside table!", "ok well let's put the bedside table between the bed and the wall then isn't it", "what you on, here you are, turn the bed the other way up and put the cabinet by the door!". An hour later we were exhausted and hysterical. Back to the first bed position we all burst out laughing and sat on the bed – the bed broke and Uncle Owen fell off the end. He bumped his head on the wall but everyone was laughing so hard we just left him there. Gran was taken to hospital and never came home.

9. June: A Fete Worse than Death!

As well as the regular youth clubs, Sunday school, weekly assemblies and lessons, there are 'one off' and annual events to prepare for. I get easily bored doing prep and much prefer working spontaneously – but then it's embarrassing when people say "Wow! You must have spent hours writing that" because I haven't, but they'll feel I didn't care how it went if I admit to not prepping. And I won't lie – so I have to spend time prepping – and get bored and irritable. This usually ends with me cleaning the bathroom, sorting the recycling, getting hair out of plug-holes, trying to sit through a bit of Lord of the Rings, and other odious tasks.

Then rushing off to the event late.

School fetes are like that, I like meeting the public and the public like what I do. They particularly like the Beatles Poem I wrote and years later several parents have approached me and said "You're that guy! The one who did the Beatles Poem, I really liked that!" (I'll include it in an appendix (2) to this book – see if you like it). When you say "I'm going to do a poem", a lot of adults glaze over, so it's best to just drop it on them with no time to switch off, then they may like it.

But the organizers of Fetes are usually in a state of panic and some have moved me to perform where no-one will see me or have not provided the mic I asked for or even forgotten that I was coming and pay me nothing. Several times I have performed and left without a word from school staff on the day or since. Weird.

That even happened in a school assembly once! I signed in and said it was my first time visit – the receptionist pointed out the hall and toilet. I set up in the hall and children began filing silently in. I played some Take That as they came in, taught them an action song and told a Bible story. The staff had all left – not one stayed to see that I was suitable or appropriate or that I could control 300 children. I finished on time and the staff returned to take their charges back to class. I left. Strange.

The theme in summer term assemblies is often “Achieving your Goal” or some similar sporting message and often I get asked to help with Sports Day. Being England most Sports Days are postponed due to bad weather at least once, some never happen! But If I can be there I fit into the background, holding the finishing line or running with a Special Needs child. When it comes to the staff race I'm sometimes asked to join in and this June achieved my all-time best position – 3rd! OK you are ahead of me now. Yes, just two other male staff.

One kid who I loved dearly insisted on running in quite a long race, despite having several problems including a leg that just wouldn't go the right way. He was fuelled by pure sunshine and beamed to the crowd as he ran – the others had long finished but I ran with him as he approached the final 100m – every eye was on him and the applause and cheers seemed to lift him shoulder high as he crossed the line. I still love that kid (man)!

Another attachment formed in a much darker circumstance and though I haven't seen the girl for many years now, the moment still haunts me. Most schools have not got their own swimming pools so when their brace of swimming lessons comes along it involves a route march to a local sports center and often I would help out with individual kids who had no water confidence at all. One child had no relationship with water at all! He was 11yrs old, had never been in a pool and clearly didn't wash either. He was fat, rude and unable to reach his feet. I helped him take his socks off while praying silently for God to give me love for this poor boy. I removed the sock from the turgid, smelly foot but the material on the sole of his feet tore away, the sock had rotted in sweat. The other sock tore and both were binned. I asked him if he took them off at night but could tell the answer was NO. He looked at me as if it was a silly question, clearly he didn't know that taking clothes off at night is a thing. I got him into the water eventually but only as the class were being told to get out of the pool to go dry off!

Several incidents in pools now come to mind, the time I fell asleep swimming a length underwater, the time my trunks split and the double incident when two kids from an informal group that had got used to walking to the pool with me got hurt (which got very complicated in A&E !).

Anyway I digressed: I have taught many kids to swim and enjoyed the sport myself up until the big accident, after that I haven't relished the thought of anything hitting my chest. Oh! I'm digressing again! Now, the girl who haunts me! Her name might have been Andrea but to me she was just a child in the pool with a class who my friend taught. I was happy to go along and on this occasion didn't go in the water. They splashed about for some minutes of free time, then he called them to the deep end for some instructions on the Badges they would be working towards. They were all confident swimmers and trod water as he talked. Then a child at the back, so towards the middle of the pool, touched the boy in front, who didn't go under but did automatically put his hand on the girl in front of him... that girl did go under slightly so reached frantically for the girl in front of her, Andrea, who had her mouth open at the time. I saw the domino effect and so did my friend the teacher. Immediately he dived in to help those now frightened little faces near the middle of the pool, I dropped onto my front, hung my shoulders over the edge and reached an arm down into the water – I grabbed Andrea and pulled. Her water covered frightened face zoomed up towards me and she came clear, I can still see that moment as I close my eyes. I lifted her out onto the side and made sure each child still in the water could get to hold the side rail.

She has no idea how scared I was for her or how precious she is to me, I guess that's just life.

One Wednesday morning, just before a big event in the afternoon, one of the Elders I was answerable to came to see how my work was going. He wanted to know how many people had been saved. I said I was sure there were people who were closer to God now than they had been but numbers were unavailable. He asked if I was challenging people enough? if I was visiting non-church people? if I was preaching the Gospel in the schools?

He was getting quite irate and a redness spread through his cheeks and above his collar line.

Suddenly he exploded! “You are not an Evangelist!” he shouted. He was in my face. I would not respond. I react negatively to loss of control – I lost respect for him and felt suddenly sad. He did not understand me or my work, perhaps my days in Basley were numbered.

After another shot across my bows he left and I had to get ready for my event in the afternoon. It felt like someone had pulled my plug out. I got changed in slow motion. The ends of my fingers began to tingle, and not in a nice way. My mind went foggy and I didn’t want to go out. Something at the back of my skull, under the bone, began to burn. I must go out, I said to myself, I must not let these people down, they don’t know what just happened and they don’t need to. Brave face on. Door open. Professional. No one knew.

That night when Mandy came home I told her and she was angry, she could see how hurt I was and wanted to ring him. No. I would do what God called me and gifted me to do and I would go when God told us to go, and not before.

Mandy got promoted soon after that, God looked after us, He always did, and He never shouted at me.

There were lighter moments: I visited a family where I had been doing Bible Study with the mum. The kids came to my Wednesday Club and went to a school I was in every week so I knew them pretty well. The lady knew Mandy so I was happy to call during the day – and on this day with the sun out and the back door open she looked the happiest I’d seen her. Life had been tough after her husband left and everything was down to her, she didn’t get a lot of sleep and the kids were demanding – but today, in a white cotton dress and the washing hanging out in the warm breeze, she looked like a woman turning a corner and seeing an ice-cream van with no queue! I went into the house and she offered me a drink of squash. She went into the kitchen to make it but then there was a shriek! I ran to the kitchen to see water on the floor, "the tap, the tap" she repeated. I'm no handyman, when I got married my tool-kit was a Swiss Army knife, but I could see the problem was under the sink unit. There was nothing for it, as water swelled on the kitchen lino, I got down on the floor, opened the cupboard doors and began emptying the household cleaning items out so I could see the pipes at the back. She squatted down next to me and took the items I passed until the area was clear. Water was now squirting directly at us, unhindered by the former contents of the cupboard and we were getting wet. As I sat on the wet floor and worked to stop the leak we were sprayed with cold water time and time again, we began laughing and giggles splashed about like the sparkling droplets that played the room – eventually I got the rubber stopper from the end of the clothes hanger on the radiator, it bunged the pipe until I could find the stop-cock and stop the water entirely. We sat on the floor, dripping, still giggling like fools, then I mopped up while she called a plumber. Happy days.

While visiting the local church-goers one day I met a man called Dave, a solidly built ex-soldier of average proportions and a gentle disposition. His face had the weathered look of experience beyond the norm and I couldn't wait to hear his story. The bungalow his family lived in was large with outhouses and sheds behind, his daughter took me round those and explained why they were filled with nineteen rabbits. I forget the reason but I also remember trying to engage his wife in conversation but she seemed a little sozzled.

There were older siblings who had moved away but this little family unit were protective and warm. Dave shared how he had been in the entertainment business on the management side and I asked about the 'stars' he had worked with and the piers he had managed around the country. There was more to Dave and we arranged to meet at a truck stop grill for lunch for a chat.

We met up and he shared more about the entertainment industry and he confided that he was struggling at home as his wife was an alcoholic and hid stashes around the house constantly. His children had left home just leaving Nicola – and she would be gone in a year or two. His heart was breaking. We arranged to meet there again in a few weeks.

10. July: Some are Coming

The last weeks of school are usually frantic. Children seem to out-grow their classrooms and Yr6 pupils seem to out-grow their schools. Teachers are often on their last legs and ask me in to cover things they've wanted to do but haven't fitted in the year so far. Sometime they ask me in to do something with Yr6 "because staff can't get them to do anything anymore".

For one sunny afternoon I had both Yr6 classes in together and had to entertain them: I asked them to write two lines of a song or poem, on any topic and in any style. I had my keyboard set up on a table and once all the lines were collected in I asked the class one by one to identify their lines – I put each to music! They loved hearing their words come to life and I changed styles to suit the mood of the lyrics. We got through about 40 of their offerings and each one I attempted was original, I didn't use anything I'd heard before. I was pleased with myself, the kids enjoyed it and the teacher came back to find it still going, so was mightily impressed.

One of the problems with church work is that after a huge and exhausting creative effort like that, you move on to the next activity where no-one knows what you have just done. It might be a service, a planning group, and afterschool club, a prayer meeting or home visit, but your mind has no time to recoil, recover and re-tune. No line-manager sees the two or three completely different creative or emotionally draining parts of your working day. There may well be an evening club or meeting to follow too, it can be relentless and unappreciated.

But the bookings kept coming in for the next academic year. And the preaching engagements stack up ahead of me. And there's another radio station that would like me to present a weekly live show. It's all exciting and great!

One Saturday I had a booking in Brighton to help with a sea-front joint churches event. A big stage had been constructed and a band was due on later. I had the big stage and small crowd all to myself. I introduced myself to some heckling, which turned out to be a seagull and launched into some jokes and magic tricks. The crowd grew, swelled by nosey passers-by, and it was clear I should do something big to present a clear Gospel message.

I had the two chairs and plank with me for the 'levitation' trick and began the Easter story that goes well with it. I got a girl from the audience to come up on the stage about the same time as the rain started and the wind began to gust. She lay on the plank over the two chairs. The awning around the scaffold stage billowed and slapped. The boards of the huge stage construction creaked, the waves far below the left side of the stage began to roar and spit. I took away the chair supporting her feet and the girl stayed still, the stage juddered and the wind blew. Then she tilted, like a burial at sea, she had the green sheet over her just as I place it over every volunteer, for effect and possible saving of modesty… she tipped with the next gust and started sliding towards the edge of the stage and the long drop to the angry waves below! I leapt forward, lifted the foot end of the girl and plank, got the chair back under her quickly and turned to the crowd. They had turned too, running for cover from the wall of rain which was now battering Brighton sea-front and dispersing the faithful. Only her family stayed and saw what happened. They laughed about it so I did too but inside I was in pieces.

Taking some time out of my school and church work I visited in the shops again and found the good traders of the mall in happier moods as the trade had picked up. I chatted with the security staff who felt that suicides were dropping and shop-lifting was on the up. I mentioned that my wife wanted a nice patio laid in our back garden but that I didn't really know here to start. The security guys were full of ideas and they offered me some tiles from the Mall – all I had to do was go down into the basement and take them home. This sounded great so at the end of the afternoon I drove my car under the shops to the "deliveries" area and pulled up by a loading bay. A huge pile of tiles, many of them marble-like in white or red, stood alone, un-regarded. A security guy passed by and helped me load some into my car. I came back another day and got 40, they were too heavy to take more.

A friend who had done patio's offered to lay them in sand for me and so our very smart garden feature began to take shape. I was several short so he offered to take me in his van and explained that if there were more spare, he'd like some for his own garden as he'd like to put in a big pool for the kids to use in the summer holidays. We went down into the bowels of the huge shopping centre and took more terrazzo tiles using his van.

On my next visit to that Mall I got chatting with one of the managers of the centre who told me that there was theft amongst the workforce and he would be cracking down on it. One of the concerns was that the replacement tiles for the shop floor levels had been slowly disappearing! I suddenly had an awful thought. I asked him to show me where the theft had occurred. Yes friends, I had been taking from the wrong pile! He showed me a little heap of broken bits and explained that the staff had been told they could take from this if they could use off-cuts and bits, but instead they had been taking the new, smart tiles from Italy!! Over two thousand pounds worth of flooring had disappeared!

My Chaplaincy badge fairly burnt into my shirt and into my skin. I had to come clean. I said I had been offered the tiles but had not understood that these smart ones were not to be touched. He was incredulous that I thought the beautiful white and red ones would be dispensed with and I humbly apologized... I offered him my patio but he was past reason. He told me to not take any more, and I decided to not tell him that my mate had a pile too.

Compliments on my nice back patio are embarrassing and I cringe every time.

Meeting up with Dave again at the truck stop grill I could immediately see trouble etched into the ever present worry lines on his rugged face.

His wife had drunk herself into a coma and was in hospital for a while. Nicola was off on work experience and he was lonely at home. Just him and 21 rabbits. He worked part time as a security guard for a large shop but that was not his mind's resting point. There was a past I wanted to know about. Before working in pier theatres he had been in army bomb disposal. He told me about the call-outs, and he chuckled as I sat horrified. After the war his team would get called out to de-fuse all sorts of explosives, unexploded bombs, dud shells, rogue mines... the legacy of warfare was scattered and surprising. Dave and the boys approached each situation as unique and every one of them could have been their last.

For a while he forgot the problems of home and drifted out into the past like a single mast boat on a clear ocean on a sunny day, with no direction and no desire for one. These were the good old days, though terrible. A safe place now, despite being the very definition of 'unsafe'!

Dave and I met again weeks later and ordered our grill. I felt a love for this guy and soon after the general chit chat of family and church we set out into the past on our little raft of memories... this time further back, before bomb disposal and marriage. He took me back to a time, just after the war when Britain was on a different footing. Rationing was still around, shortages were common, hospitals were full of the wounded and every family had a soldier or two at home looking for something that was meaningful.

Dave was Army through and through but got an assignment with the Navy, not a great combination, there would at least be some spikey banter if not actual physical hostility. Tribalism is everywhere and there are none so willing to give extreme loyalty to their group as those who have like, or have experienced, violence.

We finished our meal as Dave was recounting his voyage to the Far East with a secret team of boffins and two other army lads. The Navy were being less than welcoming and... it was time to go as Dave had to visit his wife who was still in a coma but now in a home. His love for her was undiminished despite this self-inflicted harm, she was gone really but he went almost daily to see her physical form. He would sit by her bed and think fondly and pray.

I got the phone call a few weeks later and agreed to take the service. We met at the funeral home and he took me in to see her body. She had make up on and was dressed as she would have but death had not been kind. Yet the love on his face as he gazed at her made a lasting impression on me – this was his one true love and to him she was beautiful. He cried, I tried not to and we went to the truck stop grill for lunch.

Dave's huge extended family flew in from around the globe to attend the funeral and the gathering moved on to a feast formalized by a few well-chosen and beautifully spoken words from Dave. He thanked me, but it was my honor and a real education too – I had taken several funerals and never had I seen the deceased, but I didn't let on.

The last week of term sees school groups coming to the church for leavers services and I'm involved in pulling those together, with contributions from teachers and pupils. I open up the church, set the p.a. tidy last minute obstacles and shift hundreds of chairs. They should teach "chair stacking and setting" in Bible Colleges, it's a necessary skill for all ministers and there are so many factors to be aware of, way beyond the "Health and Safety" aspects.

On the day of the Leavers Service parents will arrive up to an hour early to get a front row seat and once in they will not move for anyone, the Vicar, the disabled or even the children.

I sit nervously at the front as any number of things can and do go wrong: the microphone stand is too high/low, a child trips on the pulpit steps, a nervous kid projectile vomits and I'm the one there who knows where the mop and bucket are. Pupils cry because they don't want to leave. Pupils cry because they see others crying. Mums cry because they've been holding in tears all year and this is the moment of release, and it's ok to blub. I clear up, move the chairs back, pick up litter and equipment, shut everything down. Lock up. Feel left out.

School has finished. Joy abounds but I'm thinking about plans for Holiday Bible Club, Camp, my own holidays with family, the Assemblies to be prepared for September, the services in the holidays, the props I need for Harvest, Remembrance and Advent... I'm tired.

11. August: Away! Away!

My study is a mess, in tatters after a busy year. My nights are disturbed by nightmares of that "you are not an Evangelist" attack. My arms ache from moving chairs. I need some rest. It was over a week after the funeral of Dave's wife so we met again and had lunch – the well of experience opened up once more and Dave began to pour the cool fresh water of his adventures into my hot hands which were open to receive.

By the time our chops and onions and chips and peas arrived we were in the Pacific sun, stood on the hard grey metal deck of a battleship looking out across the blue wakeless sea towards a curved sand island. More of a sand bar really this islet was to be the base of operations for the boffins in their white coats who were burnt red under the intense sun because they were used to laboratories in England and little fresh air. They all stood and gazed at the picture. The ship was about half a mile off shore due to shallow waters and small boats were ferrying equipment from the massive gunship to the tiny lump of land encircled and highlighted by small foamy waves.

The idea was to put the scientific equipment on the land and then retreat several miles. The equipment was to monitor an explosion on a neighboring island about a mile away in the other direction. Dave and the other two army boys were there to guard the equipment on the island but currently they were still on the ship. A shed was constructed on the sand, the sort every English garden had, here it looked alone and stupid. Not a tree or bush to keep it company, it stood stark and wooden ... and obvious.

Dave knew the Russians were interested in the secret British project, no doubt they knew about the Atomic bomb too as there were many spies in the British upper classes. It was his job to keep the new science station (shed) secure, and he couldn't do it from half a mile away!

The army boys asked the Navy to take them to the island. They were told they did not have the necessary paperwork for a troop deployment. Nor could the Army disembark without permission. And they certainly couldn't steal a Navy boat to get there.

After a long argument the Navy relented, the army lads would be taken to the shore. The army lads explained it would have to be in shifts so there would be two changes of guard each 24hrs. This did not go down well.

Finally agreeing to the rotation of guards the Navy brought the scientists back from the sandy ridge in the ocean and prepared to take a soldier. The soldier asked for a gun. The Navy said no.

The Army felt, quite reasonably that if they were to stand guard on the shed in the middle of nowhere they should at least be armed. The Navy owned their guns and were not about to give any away, not without orders. Stand-off.

The army lads pleaded that the 'science station with top-secret equipment' was now exposed and vulnerable to the enemy, and this was the fault of the Navy which would be reflected in a report should an incident occur. The Navy backed down and found an old rifle they could carry. The sun beat down, the sailors in the little boat waiting by the monster battleship grew tired and still, up on deck, the verbal war continued. The Army wanted bullets.

This was an outrage. The Navy was very careful with all ammunition and the logs in the stores reflected this. They could not and would not give bullets away, not to anyone, least of all the Army!

And so it was that Dave was ferried to the tiny island to stand guard over a British shed, with a rifle but no ammunition. With days to the test explosion, the Army had to hope that if an enemy now approached the lonely science station, they did so with only one man and that he was unarmed.

Dave could see I was enthralled, too wrapped in the story to even laugh. This was like Milligan's war experiences, it was absurd, but so very British!

Our fry up devoured, like cold army rations after a long yomp, we went our separate ways. Me to pack for camp and he to go feed their 25 rabbits.

I would never normally go camping but somehow got hooked up with a crowd called Mid-Wessex Christian Camps – meeting up on the same field in the New Forest (how is it "New"? It's 700yrs old for goodness sake! Can't we at least rename it "The Middle Aged Forest"? or after a public vote call it "Leafy Tree Mac Tree Face?" or just "Colin", I don't care but the existing appellation seems inappropriate). Anyway this wonderful gang of people run a wildly exciting week for kids including great food, lots of mischief, Bible teaching and forest activities. The annual mayhem deserves another book but enough to say that the Bible is taught, worship to God is offered and the crazy is kind of infectious.

One year, for "Hunt the Officer" in New Milton, I dressed as Batman and scaled an office building (ok, just 10ft of it but the impact was visually good)– lots of middle aged women called up saucy comments about how I could come and rescue them, and that I could do something for them at home. Shame on you ladies of the New Forest!

The campers were supposed to be "hunting the officer" but they were more taken by the two Jedi Knights having a light sabre fight outside Costa Coffee and the officer dressed as Toulouse Lautrec doing an oil painting in a telephone kiosk!

Another time I dressed as a down-and-out Rasta and lay on the bench by Boots the Chemist. It was warm and the sun soaked into my black puffer jacket, my dreadlocks and woolen hat and my tatty old jeans... I dozed off. Groups of campers trawled up and down the town with their leaders, looking for disguised Camp Leaders, finding some along the way. The next thing I was aware of was a pair of smart black trousers by my face. My eyes followed the straight crease up to the start of a uniform jacket with a badge. "Allo, what 'ave we got 'ere then" said the officer who had obviously been on The Bill at some point in his non-high-flying career. I simply said "They're all after me". "Who?" he asked. "All the children" I replied, so he looked around.

At that point in the afternoon the street was fairly quiet and there were no children to be seen up or down the road! I sat up and pulled my old boots-with-no-laces on, "what have I done wrong officer?", "You are a dead body" he replied sternly. "Someone drove by Boots and called us to say there was a dead tramp on a bench – that's you sir. I'll have your full name, address and 'phone number please." I came round from my slumber and realized I could be in serious trouble, so not wanting to visit the cells for an evening I gave him the camp number too, which he rang and got verification that I was who I said and that children were indeed looking for me.

None had found me because people were scared of what I looked like and avoided me. The police lost interest but the word was out and when I returned to the field I was mobbed by laughing kids and team members who wanted to know about my arrest. I did explain that I wasn't arrested as such but they couldn't let it go – and still haven't. Great days.

The kids wake early and the officers go to bed late so it's a full on week but so worth it!

On getting home we always celebrate a great week with a take-away curry and a good film.

I take 2 days of to recover that do some planning for autumn term. Then its pack and fly off to our family escape in the sun. This year it's to Gran Canaria! We check into our lovely hotel and unpack to the sound of a family arguing in the next room.

Exploring the pools around the complex we find plenty to get excited about beyond swimming. There's a gym, an ice cream parlor and some organized games each day for the adults. Alice has a kids club each afternoon so we get a break and can be completely anonymous.

We find a lounger and settle down to the sound of a family arguing by the next bed. All Mandy and I plan to do it swim, sunbathe and read books. In the evening the kids-reps put on shows and a disco.

During our meal on the first evening two boys appear at our table. They tell me that I take assemblies in their school and one lives just two roads away from our house! How does this always happen! In Italy one time the family two rooms down in our hotel were from our town and went to school with Alice, and on our honeymoon we were sat on a coach in Switzerland with a teacher my wife knew from Bournemouth!

Each day children would come over to my sun lounger and ask for a magic trick or a joke or could I take them to the gym, we usually ended up playing cards. Ho hum. It's good to rest.

In the evenings we would eat at our balcony table and listen to the gabbling of a family arguing around the buffet. On the third night most of the Reps were off so there was to be no disco fun with the Holiday Company mascots – a big fluffy parrot, an orange fluffy cat and a soppy looking fluffy dog. I said to some of the dads that we should do the show and 2 were up for it. The missing Reps were small, fit young people, so we had to squeeze into the cartoon character costumes. Our "Green room" behind the open air stage near the bar was filled by the three of us but then we ran up the steps into the spotlights... with absolutely no idea what we were going to do next. The air had cooled to just 30 degrees and the sun was disappearing beyond the big swimming pool as we led the kids of the resort in a massive conga then staged a dance off that went on for about an hour. Those fluffy animal suits are so hot! The sweat was running down my legs into the huge foam feet and each time I jumped I landed with a squelch of warm sweat! Good times.

I returned to Basley refreshed, despite not being able to sleep on the plane because of a family arguing in the row behind, and we had a nice curry when we got home.

Several things had changed at Church: The Scottish Pastor was leaving, two other churches approached me about positions with them and my application to be on the Chaplaincy Team at the Olympics had been successful!

So a few days after the holiday, and with only a week to go before the annual 'Holiday Bible Club' I found myself planning a leaving party for the old Pastor and chairing a leaders meeting about application process for people to be on the committee to write the church profile for potential new ministers to see.

Not much fun then. But the Holiday Club was a hoot! On Day One our drummer George managed to break the front platform – the baptism pool was set into the floor and his over-enthusiastic antics caused one of the panels to split, lowering him slowly into the white tiled pool. He didn't go all the way down as he was rescued but that was just as well because the summer storms had caused the water table in our area to rise and so muddy water had come up the drain and half-filled the pool with what looked like liquid poo.

On day two, whilst acting out a Bible story I dived head first over the altar rail and came to a stop against a carved wooden cross pressing hard into my chest, everybody laughed while I coped with flashbacks to the broken sternum and that crash. Smile on. I stood, and for some reason I can't remember shouted "Bundle" … moments later I was buried in 60 children and just like one of my childhood heroes, Buster Keaton, managed to crawl out of the pile of laughing kids unnoticed. Good times.

Alice brought several friends along to the club and I noticed the boy who's leg didn't do quite what it should on Sports Day, beaming that sunshine smile as we sang songs and learned about Bible characters. Parents were staying to join in the fun too and I noticed big Barbara and one of the Elders who didn't like me.

Big Barbara was a vivacious lady with a smile to light up a city and a family to fill one. She asked the Elder next to her if she could be baptized. The Elder quizzed her and found that she had been sitting at the back of Wednesday Club listening and had come to faith! He said he would speak to me, which he did and set a date for the baptism service.

The Holiday Club over and the 60 or so children noted for future contact, we settled back into our normal routines for a few weeks until the Baptism. It's September, a great time for fresh starts and big steps. The crowds turned up, most of them Barbara's family and the church filled. The children sat around the edge of the pool which had been filled the night before and warmed by a heater for hours. I wasn't doing this one alone, another Elder joined me in the water and then Barbara descended the white tiled steps, pristine after the mud reflux incident and some repair work. The water level rose as she stood between us, the bubbling joy on her face sending ripples of excitement down her body and out in little waves to the edges of the pool. She took a gasp of breath as I said the words "Do you believe in Jesus…" then had to let it out to say "I do!" And then she went down, almost taking us down with her. We struggled to lift her up but we were soaked to the shoulders and worse still the water had been displaced and now overflowed the pool into the church – children screamed and laughed and some cried as they realized their legs and bottoms were wet. A small Tsunami made its way out from the baptistery in all directions. Barbara was now up and beaming, we all started singing her favorite worship song and parents took soggy children to the toilets to dry off. Good times.

I will always remember saying goodbye to everyone at the door and watching them walk away down the church path with wet backsides making for two-tone trousers.

Dave and I met that week and, with our shared distain for variety (except on the stage!) ordered our huge fried meals and quickly settled back into the ocean scene – the battleship now retreated, the army boys reluctantly lifted from the island and the bomb ready to explode.

Everyone wanted to watch. Every navy crewman, the three army squaddies and the officers, all lined the decks to watch the biggest man made explosion in history... perhaps.

The little shed on the tiny island was a long way ahead of them and the island about to be obliterated was well beyond that. The hundreds of onlookers stared at the horizon, squinting in the harsh sunlight.

A countdown began and an officer began a safety briefing. He said that when the bomb went off they could watch but soon after would come a blast that could be powerful. They were at that point to turn their backs to the blast and cover their faces with their hands, keeping their eyes shut.

The count-down finished and for a moment nothing happened, as if time itself had paused. Then there was a flash of silver light on the horizon followed a moment later by a trembling in the world. Then something rushing towards them. An officer shouted and they turned. Dave turned as ordered and bent his head forwards bringing his hands up and closing his eyes. The burst of hot air hit the ship and everyone on it – a foul wind of death and extreme violence.

Oddly Dave was looking at this fingers, or rather the bones in his fingers! His eyes were still shut and his hands across his face – he was seeing an x-ray of himself! This amused him and many of them shared the experience telling how it was for them over the years to come. Sadly many of those soldiers and sailors died young, of cancer. Some lived longer, many then died of cancer. The military have said it was nothing to do with the tests.

Dave misses those lads, he misses the camaraderie. They faced death, defended a shed and ever got a rifle (but no bullets!) off the Navy. Such adventures!

Dave is a hero to me, a man of several lives, much love and a serene faith in God. He did what he was given to do, did it well and laughs about it all.

12. On the Up

After the summer holidays I stayed on at Basley, through steady growth and some leadership changes. The antagonistic Elder and his wife became very critical of myself and my wife so I went to their home and apologized to them for whatever I had done to offend them. I did not judge them or ask them why, but I left silence for them to either explain or apologize for their actions or offer some refreshments. I was sincere and hurt and didn't know what to do next. They showed me the door. I had seen it before. A few weeks later they left the church! Strange.

A new Pastor came and eventually I felt it was time to move on, the church were not in a rush for me to go but agreed. Stepping into uncertainty is a matter of faith, and God always has a plan though it is often invisible at first. After leaving the Church I filled the time working at a local airport. Chairs keep breaking under me, bizarre and wonderful people latch onto me. Mandy and Alice continued to amaze and delight me. Curry is still a thing – see Appendix 3.

I'll leave the tales of tree felling, a woman who sank 3 ships, airport emergencies and Olympic Chaplaincy for another day and perhaps another book. All these stories are true though shaped into a single year for ease of reading and with some identifying details changed. I hope you have enjoyed a sample of my life and I thank you for sharing it.

Appendix 1

Babel

Many wonder why they do it,
Those explorers who love the extreme
They constantly push the boundaries
Looking for death, or so it would seem,
Well I think I have found the answer
And it lies in the ancient book
It's a story told in Genesis, just pause and have a look.

The architectural folly, or mythical tower some would say,
Was to be the tallest ever, a grand claim even today!
The people wanted to reach the sky those many millennia ago,
They didn't know what was up there
 but the sun and rain and snow.
Their aim was to reach to God above, to be as strong as Him,
Perhaps then they would feel no need to pray,
Would Heaven open and let them in?
They never finished the edifice,
God knew they wouldn't survive,
Without the right technology,
Collapse would leave few alive.

So he hampered their communication,
And with the project running late,
The tower was not completed,
Because they couldn't co-operate.

But that was then and this is now –
 so have we learned so very much?
Just Google skyscrapercity.com a click, a drag, a touch,
Will reveal that man is just the same,
Competitively building towers,
The projects are in open files, I look at them for hours!
In China and Arabia the tallest almost fly,
Man has much new technology and will go higher by and by…
A "Supertall" is 1,000ft a "Megatall" twice that,
But "Hypertall's" are on their way,
Just read the engineer's chat.

The sky, once thought the limit,
Was nothing of the sort,
And man has already been further,
So what is the driving thought?
The Burj Dubai is tallest now (as in 2017 I write)
And the Jeddah Tower is rising, but have they got God in sight?
They are built on sand and look so grand,
It's a race! Is that surprising?
And it's not only up but down they go,
Risking life and limb the same,
The deepest mine, the longest cave,
But it's much more than a game…
It's a human trait to risk ourselves,
To find things to overcome,
To push the farthest limits,
Appeals, to not all, but some.

Don't tell me I can't do that, don't say it can't be done,
Im human and I'll do it – rebellion 1 – 0 – 1
I'll circumnavigate the earth, why? To show I can!
I'll fly up to the moon and back – will this improve a man?
(If we land on Mars and plant potatoes there one day,
Will we be as one with God above,
will there be no need to pray?)

Extremes are not a new fashion,
they're just more reachable now,
But all they show is our smallness, our frailty,
In a vast universe of - WOW!

T.J. Hill
16 February 2017

Appendix 2

The Beatles Poem

A Reading from the Second part of the 20th chapter of the Gospel of St John Lennon.

And the gift was upon them and they did write unto the young men and the daughters of men as the voice of those crying in the stadium Love, Love Me Do, and the people did love them greatly except those who did love them not.

And they did give generously saying From Me To You but Please Please Me because I Want to Hold Your Hand, but though She Loves You, Money Cannot Buy Me Love and so I Saw Her Standing There and she did Twist And Shout, and protested much.

And so St George, who never slew a dragon but did inflict much damage upon many ears and countless guitars did ask in a letter: Do You Want to Know a Secret? and did end saying PS I Love You and in the writing of it was much toil for A Hard Day's Night for he said Ain't She Sweet And I Love Her, but where did the Ringo ?

And he sighed ah yes it is in this Matchbox and I Feel Fine.

And discernment was made but in the reckoning thereof was much error for St John said She's a Woman Eight Days a Week and She's Got a Ticket to Ride as a Day Tripper but Help - it was for Yesterday !

And so the fab four were lonesome having not sought God's direction and became headstrong saying We Can Work It Out and one became a Paperback Writer but it got him Nowhere Man and he did plan to escape down Penny Lane through Strawberry Fields and onto a Yellow Submarine with Eleanor Rigby.

But the four could not agree and said All You Need Is Love but then again Hello Goodbye and were not friends – and some sought God on a Magical Mystery Tour and did lead millions of their disciples into the wilderness and there was much weeping and wailing and many did turn around and reject their former ways. And they prayed to the Son of the Lady Madonna and asked what they should read and God said Hey! Jude and so there was a Revolution and many said let us Get Back to the ways of God and they said to the Lord, Got To Get You Into My Life, and the Lord said do you still believe the Ballad of John and Yoko ? Are the Beatles greater than Jesus? Now Come Together and follow the right path, it will not be easy as it is a Long and Winding Road such as found Back in the USSR but if you Love Me, Do know I will guard and keep your Rubber Soul.

And the saved ones found life to be Something New and meaningful and they with one voice cried Let It Be! and were no more counted amongst Sgt. Pepper's Lonely Hearts Club Band for they were Free Like a Bird and they knew that the Apple had been sinful.

Tim Hill
12 January 1996

Appendix 3

Towards A Biblical Theology of Curry

On the 5th day (or period) of creating, God had put everything in place – the stars in their places and the earth exactly positioned for heat and light within acceptable tolerances.

But no creature as yet to appreciate a good curry. So He kept on creating. The curry plant and spices were growing nicely but no animal could so far be found that would ingest the range of tastes available. Until humanity came about – then He stopped. He could have gone on... we can only wonder what better creatures would have resulted... but it was enough. Humanity would make and enjoy curry, job done!

The Fall – (or Phall ?)

Adam and Eve walked and talked with God in the cool of the evening and were swapping vegetarian recipes when Cain and Able, their sons made dishes and brought them as offerings to God.

It seems reasonable then to assume that God was taking human form to walk with them. Probably a similar form each day so He could be familiar to them. They lived many hundreds of years due to a good diet of vegetable and fruit based dishes (e.g. Malaya) and the total lack of anything bad, like processed meat, high alcohol content drinks or fried Mars Bars.

There would have been spicy stew from the earliest of times, archaeologists have found suitable bowls, and so Korma, and Masala were no doubt popular.

There was one particular tree which God was keeping special – producing a chilli with real fire to it – but Adam and Eve ate that one night and really regretted it in the morning. Everything changed. A ring of fire around the Garden of Eden and a fear of facing God for a nice walk. They felt guilty and yet wanted more. They made aprons of fig leaves because they soon found out the punishment for touching the chilli then touching private parts was extremely harsh.

Once banned from the Garden the young family found life tougher. They had to farm to get ingredients to cook, planted up paddy fields with and often disagreements cropped up.

Cain killed Abel over a vegetable Korai while Adam started adding chicken to his tikka and Eve missed those cooling evening walks so invented Raitha.

After many generations had come and gone the population had grown to tens of thousands and every family had their preferred recipes. Fights broke out in market places and spices from further east multiplied the choices, Rezala, Madras, Vindaloo... and mankind could not cope with all these options. The only answer was to take sides and go to war. Many of them were killed and the rest ate Weetabix. This was the final straw – God decided to turn the world into a great big wok, mix everything up and start again.

Noah took a lot of chickens on board and good job too. No, I'm not saying Job was on the ark, he might have even lived before the Flood seeing that in his book he mentions various dinosaurs and they don't seem to have been around after the deluge. But he probably cooked them up as he had a large family – you can imagine a Brontosaurus and Plesiosaur Mixed Meat Tandoori would have made a feast for Jobs whole clan and farm workers as well. NB BBQ ribs caused a number of crushing fatalities and were banned for health and safety reasons.

Anyway we come to recent history – just about 4,000yrs ago and a man named Abraham. He lived in Ur and didn't like it much so didn't take much persuading to leave. God told him to pack his spices and take the family on a trek, to boldly go where no chef had gone before... up the Euphrates and down into Haran. His dad died there after a particularly good Lamb Rogan Josh and the rest of the family carried on to Egypt where the King had cooks that could make spiced goat and couscous seem almost as appetising as a meat Jalfrezi !

Abraham's son Isaac loved spicy food – Meat Jalfrezi Masala appears to have been his favourite – and his crafty son Jacob cooked one just like his older brother Esau used to make. Isaac was fooled by this culinary deception and gave Jacob his Blessing. Because of that curry Jacob and his descendants the Jews got to be dominant over the other tribes in the Middle-East and the arguing about that has not stopped since. It's not an overstatement to say that the fraudulent offering of Jacobs curry changed world history.

What is it? (Hebrew: Manna)

After becoming slaves in Egypt the Jews got out with the help of a spicy lamb curry (Passover) and an angel who slew the elder child of each Egyptian family (well, all who didn't eat the curry). Pharaoh let them go and then changed his mind – those Egyptians eh?! Moses led the Jews through the Red Sea and into the desert. They developed their mobile kitchens there and made money by selling samosas and bhaji's to passing traders.

After 40yrs of going round the desert then around the wilderness near the Dead Sea they must have wondered if it was all leading to something big – it was, the Promised Land! But they were not ready yet, there was much to learn. While complaining about the lack of fresh water, the lack of bread and the lack of meat (think back to school dinners – ugh!) they were read the riot act by Moses.

God saved them again, this time with Naan bread and Poppadum's – small white bread-like food appeared all around the camp in huge quantities! No one knew what it was thus the name "Manna" (literally "what is it?") but it was a hit and joined the regular diet from that time on.

Kings and things

The Jews (or Hebrews or Israelites or Invaders [you choose]) developed their cooking into an art-form and settled the land in twelve sections to concentrate on the essentials: Starters, Tikkas, Bhuna's, Biryani's, Balti's, Madras's, Jalfrezi's, Vindaloo's, Faal's, Breads, Rices & extras, foreign food.

The Kings, Saul then David then Solomon increased in knowledge and wealth as the culinary power-house of the world made Jerusalem its capital and formed an army to protect its borders and lists of ingredients. It was probably Solomon, famed for his unprecedented wisdom, who designed the perfect curry – the Cingari (or Chingari or Cinghari [you choose but don't get upset this time]).

Next the country split north and south like a lentil! Kings Jerry and Ray slugged it out and later kings totally wrecked the country. Eventually Assyria swept in, fuelled by delicate spices in their goat curry and then Babylon came in the next wave of terror, and for a while the area was all destruction and doner kebabs.

Exiled to the Euphrates area the Jews had to use the milder techniques to serve the new master race – the Persians – and one vegetarian option served by Daniel went down particularly well. Their flavour was in favour and their status began to rise. The most notable hic-up was as a result of a brief foray into the idea of layered pasta – Belshazzar's Feast was found wanting - a disaster for everyone.

Getting another crack at running the Promised Land the Jews returned and got cooking again... welcoming surprise guests over the coming years such as the Greeks, the Romans and some radical insurgents. The country was a huge melting-pot of cultures now and everyone stayed because they liked the aroma in the streets of the towns and cities – fresh curry was in the air!

The Last Curry

Despite people getting the year and date of His birth wrong the Son of God was not going to be ignored. He would invite himself to tea, produce loaves and fish curry, make great wine and even forgave people who didn't like mango Chutney!

Just before He died He sat the disciples and other followers down and laid on a Lamb Rogan Josh – He dipped the Peshawari Naan into it with one of the lads, Judas, who started to choke on it and had to confess he was about to desert to the other side (no, not Vegans). Again a turning point in history as the Lord said all His followers for the rest of history should take the bread (or Naan or Poppadum [you choose carefully]). Catholics liked the thin wafer whereas Anglicans preferred the flat bread and non-conformists used their loaf – thus another lot of arguing ensued. He said eat it together regularly until He returns. So we do.

And that's why the world is like it is.

Tim Hill
16 February 2018

www.ingramcontent.com/pod-product-compliance
Ingram Content Group UK Ltd.
Pitfield, Milton Keynes, MK11 3LW, UK
UKHW020241250726
13967UKWH00001B/499

9 781905 691678